MYTHS OF THE WORLD

CLASSICAL DEITIES AND HEROES

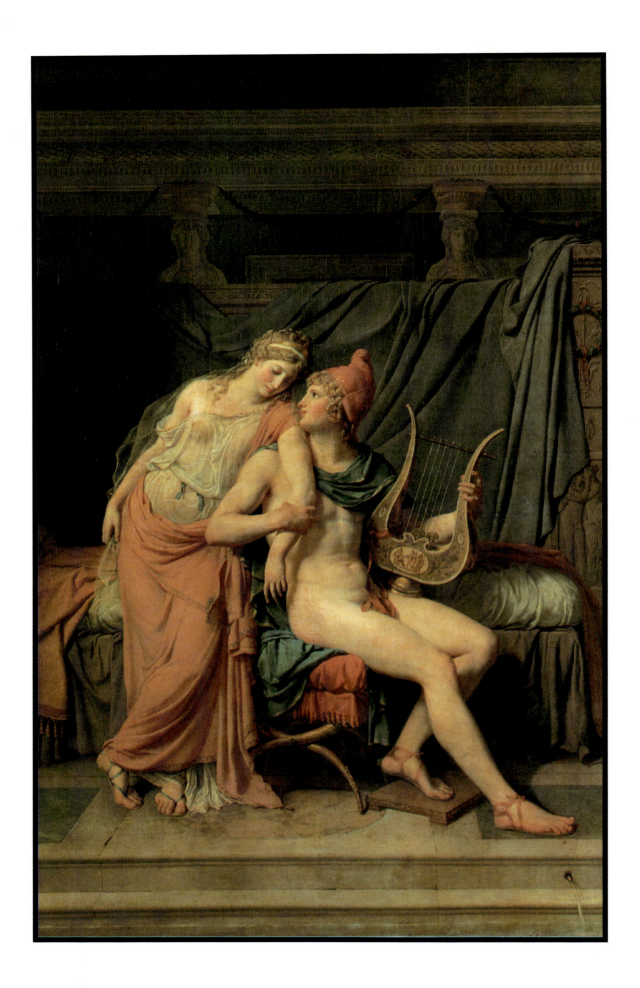

MYTHS OF THE WORLD

CLASSICAL DEITIES AND HEROES

MORGAN J. ROBERTS

MetroBooks

MetroBooks

An Imprint of Friedman/Fairfax Publishers

© 1995 by Michael Friedman Publishing Group, Inc.

The Library of Congress has previously cataloged this book as follows:

Roberts, Morgan J., 1970–
    Classical deities and heroes / Morgan J. Roberts
        p.   cm. — (Myths of the world)
    Includes bibliographical references (p.110) and index.
    ISBN 1-56799-089-4
    1. Mythology, Classical. I. Title.   II. Series.
BL782.R62 1994
292. 1'3—dc20   94-10307
                                                   CIP

Editor: Benjamin Boyington
Art Director: Jeff Batzli
Designer: Susan E. Livingston
Photography Editor: Susan Mettler

Color separations by Scantrans Pte. Ltd.
Printed in China by Leefung-Asco Printers Ltd.

For bulk purchases and special sales, please contact:
Friedman/Fairfax Publishers
Attention: Sales Department
15 West 26th Street
New York, NY 10010
212/685-6610 FAX 212/685-1307

PHOTOGRAPHY CREDITS

Alinari/Art Resource, New York: 85

Art Resource, New York: 48

Bridgeman/Art Resource, New York: 16

Giraudon/Art Resource, New York: 2, 20, 38, 62, 65, 86, 89, 95, 105 bottom left and right

Kavaler/Art Resource, New York: 49

Erich Lessing/Art Resource, New York: 6, 8, 11, 12, 14, 15, 19, 22, 26, 34, 37, 40, 54, 55, 60, 61, 76, 79, 90, 92, 96, 97, 103, 107, 108

Nimatallah/Art Resource, New York: 58

North Wind Picture Archives: 28 bottom, 29 both, 43 left, 50, 52, 53 top, 70, 72 right, 73, 74, 75, 84, 99

Scala/Art Resource, New York: 10, 18, 24, 25, 28, 32–33, 35, 36, 42, 47, 52, 56, 59, 64, 66–67, 68, 71, 80, 82, 88 bottom, 100, 102, 104, 109

Thessalonike Museum/Art Resource, New York: 30

Werner Forman Archive/Art Resource, New York: 44

DEDICATION

For Pop, for getting me interested in mythology in the first place.

ACKNOWLEDGMENTS

Thanks to Amy Bohlman for her patience through the writing of this book and to Ben Boyington for his skill, advice, and friendship.

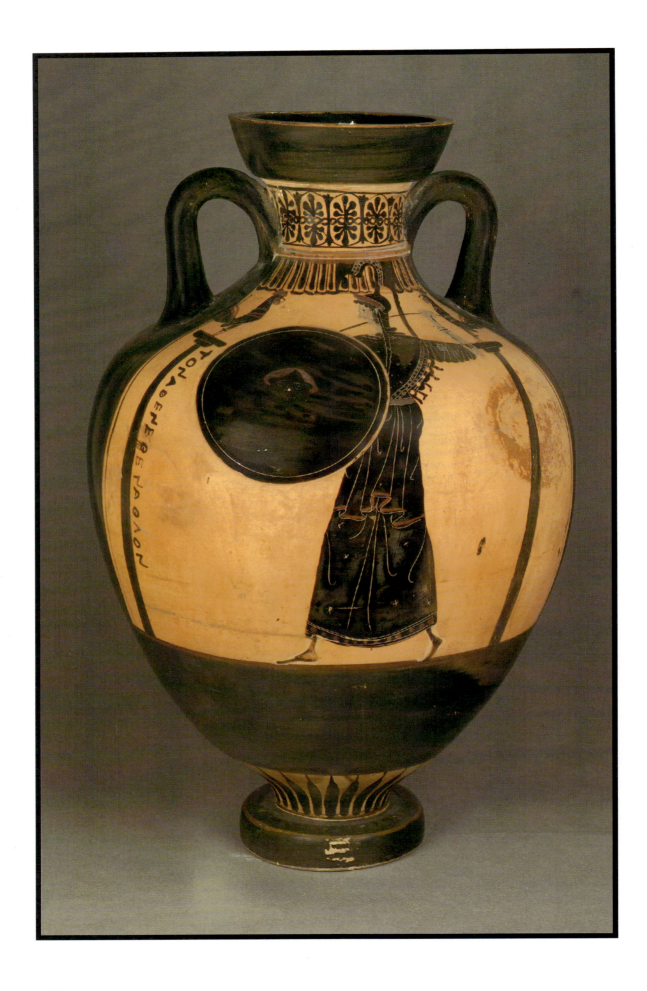

CONTENTS

8 CHAPTER I: THE CREATION OF THE UNIVERSE

12 CHAPTER II: THE REIGN OF KRONOS

16 CHAPTER III: THE CREATION OF MAN

22 CHAPTER IV: ZEUS AND HERA

26 CHAPTER V: POSEIDON—GOD OF THE OCEANS

30 CHAPTER VI: HADES AND DEMETER

38 CHAPTER VII: APHRODITE AND ARES

44 CHAPTER VIII: APOLLO AND ARTEMIS—
THE TWINS OF JUSTICE

50 CHAPTER IX: ATHENA AND HEPHAESTUS—
ARCHITECTS OF CIVILIZATION

56 CHAPTER X: HERMES AND DIONYSUS

62 CHAPTER XI: THE LESSER OLYMPIANS

68 CHAPTER XII: THE QUEST FOR THE GOLDEN FLEECE

76 CHAPTER XIII: THE TWELVE LABORS OF HERACLES

86 CHAPTER XIV: THE TROJAN WAR

100 CHAPTER XV: THE TRAVELS OF ODYSSEUS

110 GREEK AND ROMAN NAMES

110 BIBLIOGRAPHY

111 INDEX

CHAPTER

I

THE
CREATION OF THE
UNIVERSE

According to Greek mythology, the universe was spawned from a great, limitless abyss devoid of form or content, an area of continual confusion and unrelenting darkness. This was Chaos, the progenitor of all things. Out of it came all aspects of the classical universe: the gods, the monsters, the earth, and man.

Chaos gave birth to, and subsequently was lord over, three entities: Erebus, the primeval darkness; Nox, the deepest night; and Eros, the unbridled

Detail from Greek sculpture, 2nd century B.C.,
showing Athena (left) fighting Gaea's sons
while Gaea (bottom right) emerges from below
to tend to her fallen children.

9

reproductive urge. Along with Chaos, these entities were the only things to exist in the universe for untold ages.

The next entity to come into being was Love, the child of Erebus and Nox. Without question, Eros had a hand in Love's creation, for without Eros, the urge to reproduce would never have overtaken Erebus and Nox. (In later myths there is another character named Eros who is a more anthropomorphic version, a more limited and understandable characterization of this primordial reproductive force.) Once Love had been created, there was no way that Chaos could continue its reign—Love began to order and harmonize the haphazard nature of the universe.

Eventually Love gave birth to the primary forces of Light and Day. These two siblings were able to vanquish disorder and create an environment ripe for the spontaneous creation of Gaea (Earth) and Uranus (Heaven).

With the advent of Gaea and Uranus, we begin to see the emergence of the first true characters of classical mythology. During their reign, Uranus and Gaea had five distinct types of children, all of whom Uranus treated rather poorly. It was Uranus' mistreatment of his offspring that eventually led to his downfall.

Their first three children were extremely strong, gargantuan monsters with a hundred hands and fifty heads each. These creatures were called the Hekatoncheires, or the Hundred-handed Ones. As soon as they were born, Uranus, filled with disgust, imprisoned them beneath the earth. Next to emerge from Gaea were the Cyclopes, another hideous race, easily recognizable by the one large eye in the center of their heads. Like the Hekatoncheires, these creatures were mountainous in size and possessed terrifying power. Unlike the Hundred-handed Ones, however, they were allowed to roam the earth as they pleased.

The last intentional children to come from Gaea and Uranus were the Titans, who, apart from their tremendous size and strength, were not the monsters their brethren were. They were twelve in number, consisting of six males—Coeus, Hyperion, Iapetus, Krios, Kronos, and Oceanus—and six females—Mnemosyne, Phoebe, Rhea, Theia, Themis, and Tethys. As he did with the Cyclopes, Uranus allowed the Titans to wander the earth at will.

Gaea was outraged that her husband would punish the Hekatoncheires simply because of their appearance. In her matriarchal fury she convinced the Titans that justice was due and that they should rebel against their father. Kronos, the leader of the Titans, ambushed Uranus and castrated him, stripping

The Castration of Uranus by Kronos, Georgio Vasari, c. 1555–1559.

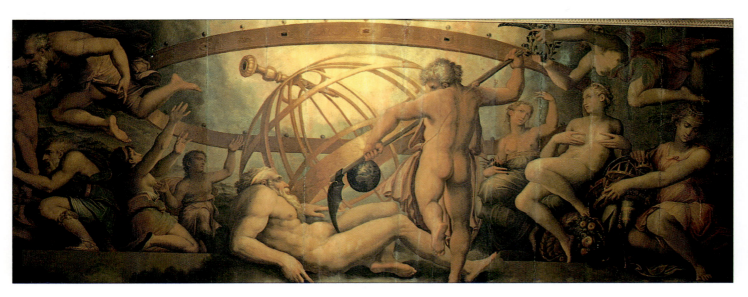

The Fall of the Giants, fresco, Giulio Romano, c. 1532–1534.

him of his power. The blood from Uranus' wounds fell upon Gaea and was transformed into the last two pre-Olympian races: the Giants and the Erinnyes.

The Giants would prove to be continual adversaries for the race of gods still to come, the Olympians, although their attacks never gained them anything more than numerous wounds and the shame of defeat. The three Erinnyes (or Furies) were, for mortal man at least, the most terrible of all the pre-Olympians. It was the job of these blind, winged, birdlike sisters to torment those guilty of crimes against the social order, particularly blood-crimes against the family and murder. The Erinnyes were horrible creatures with their hair entwined with countless serpents. They wielded whips and hurled fire against their enemies. Because of their blindness, the Erinnyes couldn't tell when their victims had been suitably punished, and the victims often went insane because of this continual torture and were driven to kill again.

With the castration of Uranus, and Kronos' subsequent ascension to the throne, the reign of the first cycle of gods came to an end, and the stage was set for Kronos (Time) to rule the world with his wife and sister, Rhea.

THE
REIGN OF KRONOS

Some time after his reign began, Kronos learned of a prophecy that one of his children would overthrow him in much the same way he had overthrown his father. In an attempt to forestall this, he devised a simple plan: He would eat each of his children the moment they were born. Although she was overwhelmed with grief, Rhea was powerless to stop her husband and could only stand by and watch while Kronos devoured their first five children, the gods Demeter, Hades, Hera, Hestia, and Poseidon. Before their sixth child—

Relief of 7th century B.C. sculpture from the
Temple of Artemis in Corfu, Greece,
depicting Zeus fighting Kronos.

the infant Zeus—was born, however, Rhea had devised a plan that would save him. Immediately after his birth, she wrapped a stone in swaddling clothes and gave this to Kronos in place of the child. The Titan swallowed the bundle, thinking he had once again averted his deposal. Meanwhile, Rhea carried the infant to Mount Ida, on the island of Crete, where she placed him in the care of the Curetes (spirits of indeterminate origin).

The Curetes were a warrior race who were masters of bronze weaponry. In order to hide the cries of the infant Zeus from Kronos' ears, they continuously danced a wild war dance, clashing their swords and shields together,

creating a furious cacophony. In later myths, the Curetes were credited with endowing the Cretans with the knowledge of both metallurgy and agriculture.

Since Rhea could not come to Crete regularly to feed her young son, the she-goat Amaltheia nourished the young god in her stead. It was Amaltheia's hide that eventually covered the Aegis, Zeus' all-protective shield, and it was one of her horns, after it broke off, that was transformed by Zeus into the Cornucopia—a magical horn that would become filled with whatever its possessor wished.

During the time Zeus was on Crete, his companion and teacher was Metis, a daughter of the Titans Oceanus and Tethis. The word *metis* means "wisdom," and wisdom is exactly what Metis brought to the young Zeus. As his teacher, she taught him the ways of the world and provided him with the means to overthrow his father. Later, as Zeus' first consort, she literally filled him with all the wisdom she herself personified.

When Zeus was fully grown, he decided that it was time he replaced Kronos as the lord of the heavens. Unfortunately, although he was full of desire, he had no concrete plans. Metis gave him a potion that, she said, would force Kronos to vomit up the five swallowed children still living in his stomach. With the help of Rhea, Zeus was able to trick Kronos into drinking the elixir, and Zeus' five brothers and sisters were soon free. When they came back into the world, they were furious at their father, and Zeus had no trouble convincing them to combine their forces and help Zeus to achieve Kronos' overthrow.

Thus began the war between the Titans and the Olympians. Of all wars, there is none so destructive as that between immortals, for in a conflict of this kind there can be no casualties—the fallen will quickly rise again, completely healed, to continue the battle. Such was the war between the Titans and the Olympians; had not Zeus enlisted the aid of some formidable allies, this war might have caused the destruction of the earth itself.

Hoping to turn the tide of battle to his advantage, Zeus freed the Hundred-handed Ones from their prison in Tartarus. Indebted to the young god, these monsters gladly agreed to add their earthshaking power to the forces assembled against the Titans. The Cyclopes also allied themselves with Zeus, supplying him with the arsenal of thunder and lightning that would later become his

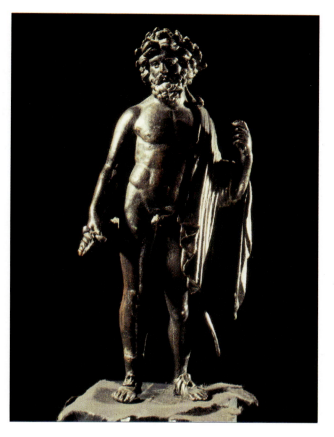

trademark weapons. With the ranks of their relatively young army now bolstered, Zeus and the Olympians soon defeated the Titans. Much as Kronos had done to Uranus countless ages before, Zeus castrated his father. He then imprisoned the Titans in the bowels of the earth.

With the Titans now vanquished, the question of leadership arose, with each of the three male Olympians—Hades, Poseidon, and Zeus—vying for the position. Even though Zeus had freed them from their father's stomach and masterminded his overthrow, Hades and Poseidon still thought of him as their younger brother, and therefore not suited to the position of supreme ruler. Since there were two other areas in need of rulers, the oceans and the underworld, the three decided to draw lots. Hades became ruler of the underworld; Poseidon was made sovereign over the oceans; and Zeus was granted reign over all else, becoming the king of the gods. The age of the Olympians had begun.

THE
CREATION OF MAN

After all of the original Olympians were born and Zeus usurped the throne, it was time for man to come into being. In the classical canon there are two versions of the ascent of mankind; in both versions, the Titan Prometheus plays an important role.

In the first version, men were said to grow from the earth like grain. In this account, the gods oversaw five different generations, or ages, of man that became less perfect with each successive age.

Prometheus Carrying Fire, Jan Crossiers,
17th century.

pick. One portion con-
tained the tender meat, but
Prometheus covered this share
with the hide of the ox, making it ap-

RIGHT: Black-figured
kylix, c. 555 B.C.,
depicting two of the
early punishments of
Zeus: Atlas supporting
the world, in
retaliation for leading
an unsuccessful coup
against Zeus, and
Prometheus having
his liver eaten
by the eagle.

OPPOSITE: Marble relief
from a Roman
sarcophagus,
A.D. 3rd century,
showing Prometheus
creating man. Behind
the Titan stands
Minerva (the Roman
version of Athena)
guiding him in
this endeavor.

The first generation was called the Golden Age. Although mortal, the men of this age
lived as carefree a life as the gods: Food and
drink were abundant; hardship and strife were
unknown; and when death finally took them,
they became the guardian angels of mankind.
The men of the Golden Age lived in harmony
with the gods, with the two races at times
even sharing the same table. It was during one
of these banquets that Prometheus played a
trick on Zeus that the king of the gods did not
appreciate—his resultant wrath led to the end
of the Golden Age.

As the table was being prepared, Prometheus slew an ox and divided it into two portions, of which the gods were to have first

pear unappetizing and stringy. The other portion contained nothing more than bones, but
was covered with tantalizing layers of rich fat.
Zeus immediately chose the fat-covered, tasty
portion, thus giving the fulfilling meat to the
mortals. When Zeus, who was never known
for his cool head, discovered this deception,
he became enraged and decreed that from
that point on man would no longer be free of
hunger and would no longer be permitted to
use fire, which cooked the meat and made it
edible. From now on, man would have to toil
furiously in the fields, spending all his time
planting and harvesting the grain that until
then had grown without aid.

Feeling guilty, Prometheus flew to the sun
and stole some of its fire, which he brought

to earth, hid in the stem of the fennel plant, and gave to man. This fire, however, was not as perfect as the fire of the Golden Age—it had as delicate a life as man, and would die if not attended constantly.

Zeus soon learned of Prometheus' transgression. Always prone to violent retaliation, Zeus decided to punish not only Prometheus but man as well. Prometheus was chained to a rock in the Caucasus Mountains where every day a ravenous eagle would tear open his belly and devour his liver. This ghastly wound would heal overnight, just in time for the eagle's next visit. Man's punishment, though less violent, was no less painful. Up to this point, man had lived without women; new men grew from the ground, much like wheat, and when they died, they died peacefully, without pain. Sickness, plague, feebleness—all these things were unknown to them, as were heartbreak, lust, and deception.

Zeus ordered that a "gift" be made for man. This gift had the form of the goddesses and was endowed by different deities with different traits. Aphrodite, the goddess of physical love, graced the creation with a beauty that would instill lust in the hearts of man. Athena, the goddess of wisdom, gave the gift the knowledge of how to care for man. Hermes, the god of thievery and cunning, granted the creation the ability to lie. Zeus' gift was named Pandora, and she was the first woman.

Zeus sent Pandora to earth. Upon her arrival, men became helplessly enthralled by her beauty. From this point on, man was not alone on the earth; there was now something that would arouse his desires and make his mind stray from whatever he was doing. In order to have children, he would have to take time away from his crops and his animals to woo her and convince her that he was worthy of her affections.

Eva Prima Pandora,
Jean Cousin,
c. 1530–1560.

Pandora also brought with her an infamous piece of luggage: a box that Zeus had ordered her never to open. Curiosity soon got the better of her and she lifted the lid just a little. Out of the tiny crack flew all the evils and pestilence that contaminate the world; Painful Death, Suffering, Disease, Plague, Jealousy, Hatred, Envy, Crime—all these demons and more flew from the box. Terrified, she slammed the lid back down, but it was too late. She'd been able to keep only one of the box's residents inside; if Hope had escaped as well, mankind would have nothing to believe in during times of hardship. Thus the Golden Age of man came to an end.

The men of the Silver Age were decidedly less intelligent than those of the Golden Age. This lack of intelligence, coupled with all the pain and suffering released by Pandora, made the Silver Age a time of great hardship. Men would fight each other over trifles. But because their intelligence was so low, or perhaps their worries so great, they were never able to do anything more than fight small battles among themselves.

Such was not the case with the Brass Age. The men of this age had had the time to grow accustomed to the evils released by Pandora and hence were of a sturdier stock. This proved to be their downfall. They banded together into groups and waged war against others of their own kind. The Brass Age was an age of brutality, a time during which men forgot that they were brothers. This generation soon killed itself off with countless violent wars and blood feuds.

The next era was the Bronze Age, the age of the greatest heroes of classical mythology. This was the age that supplied the stories that poets and storytellers would recount throughout the ages—in *The Iliad* and *The Odyssey*, the great poet Homer would tell of the famous Bronze Age heroes Achilles and Odysseus. The Bronze Age was the time of Jason and the Argonauts and the demigod Heracles. It was a time of legend and greatness.

The last age, the Iron Age, was the time during which ancient Greek civilization as we know it flourished. It was an age dominated by the seductiveness of power, a corrupt age during which good was easily put aside for personal gain, and a time when the lines between good and evil were blurred and confused.

The second version of the creation of man again has Prometheus, this time with his brother Epimetheus, playing an important role.

The two brothers were complete opposites. Prometheus, whose name means "foresight," was level-headed, while Epimetheus, whose name means "afterthought," was prone to acting without thinking.

After the war with the Titans, the job of creating the earth's inhabitants was entrusted to these two brothers. Epimetheus was the first to act, diving into the act of creation without much preparation. He created the animals first, endowing them with the qualities needed to survive in a harsh, unforgiving environment, such as speed, agility, and strength. He also gave the animals their hides, wings, fins, and shells, but left nothing to protect man, his final creation. Being true to his name, Epimetheus looked back on what he had done and realized he'd made a terrible mistake. He went to his brother for help.

Prometheus, taking stock of the situation, believed that man could be salvaged. He made man stand upright, in the posture of the gods, making him tower over the animals. He also gave man fire from the sun, which not only would provide protection from all the beasts, but would enable him to warm his furless body, even on the coldest of nights.

In both versions, with the aid of Prometheus, man came to master fire, and he subsequently became the master of the tiny globe he called home.

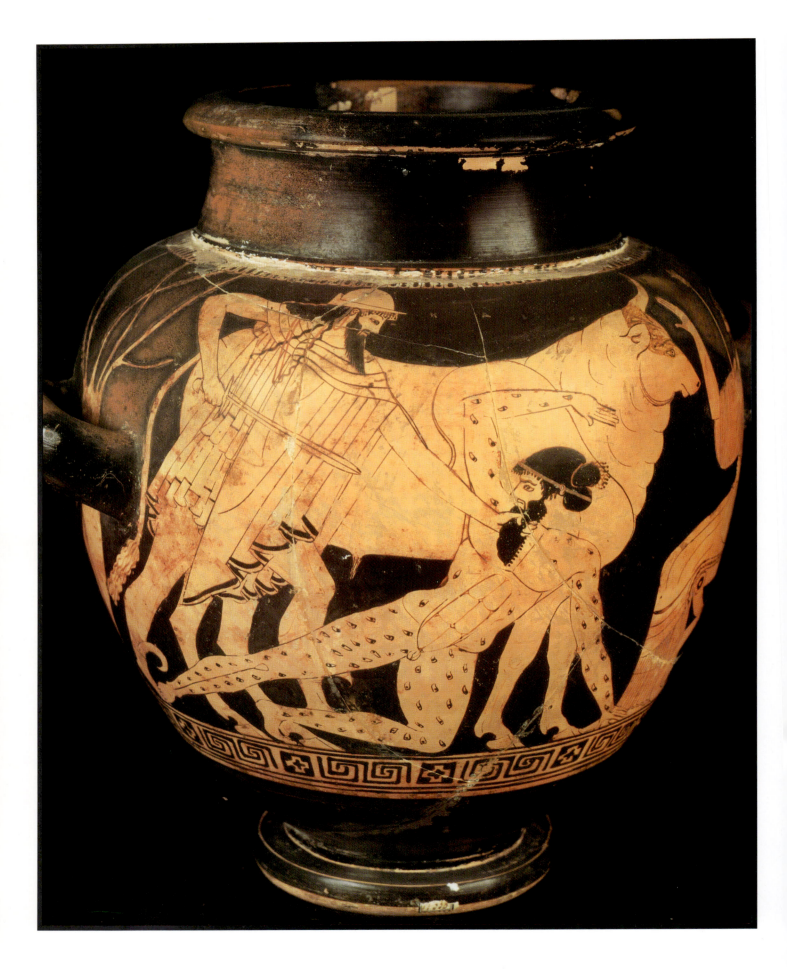

ZEUS
AND HERA

ZEUS—KING OF THE GODS

As supreme ruler of both Olympus and the world beneath it, Zeus was the most powerful god in classical mythology. He controlled such primal forces as thunder and lightning, and had the power to squeeze the clouds together, forcing them to feed the earth with nourishing rain.

Besides his terrible power, Zeus possessed the Aegis, an impervious piece of armor. In different myths, the Aegis appears in different forms, the most com-

Red-figured stamnos, 5th century B.C., depicting Hermes slaying Argus, the hundred-eyed guardian of Io. On the far right, the arm and leg of Zeus are visible.

23

mon being that of a shield or breastplate covered with Almaltheia's hide. In some myths, the Aegis is a thundercloud. Whatever its form, the Aegis always has the same purpose: to protect Zeus from any foe, mortal or otherwise. When shaken, it produces a mighty thunderstorm, sending terror and fear into the hearts of Zeus' enemies. Of all his attributes, the Aegis most clearly depicts Zeus' unparalleled power.

Despite Zeus' status as the most powerful Olympian, he also had his share of human characteristics. The ancient Greeks believed Zeus to be a rather promiscuous god. The exact number of his lovers would be staggering if it could be calculated. It seems he was always either in the middle of an affair or calculating his next seduction. Most of his children were conceived not with his wife, Hera, but with the women with whom he had his countless affairs.

Even as a young god on the island of Crete, his desires had a strong hold on him. His first conquest was Metis, the daughter of Oceanus and Tethys and the personification of wisdom. When Metis became pregnant, Uranus and Gaea warned their grandson that the child born to Metis might grow to be greater than Zeus in both power and wisdom. Zeus felt he had no choice but to swallow both Metis and her unborn child, ending the possible threat to his future rule. As a result, Zeus was literally filled with wisdom, a trait the king of the gods must possess, and was made "pregnant" with the goddess Athena, who, some time later, emerged fully armed and fully grown from the head of Zeus.

Bust of Juno, Roman copy after Greek original. Juno was the Roman name for Hera.

By other "companions," Zeus fathered such gods and demigods as Apollo, Artemis, Hermes, Aphrodite (in some versions), Dionysus, Heracles, Helen of Troy, and Persephone. Many of the most famous Greek heroes were illegitimate children of Zeus, and many of the great families of ancient times claimed to have at least one direct descendant of Zeus somewhere on their family trees.

HERA— QUEEN OF THE GODS

Wife and sister of Zeus, and daughter of Kronos and Rhea, Hera was the goddess of the family, of familial love, and of legitimate childbirth. Since Hera was the personification of marital fidelity, Zeus' constant philandering angered her to no end. Her jealousy was so great that she kept a continual eye on her husband. When she discovered an infidelity, she would become so enraged that Zeus' lover, and at times the offspring of their coupling, would soon suffer her wrath.

THE MYTH OF IO— CONSEQUENCES OF OLYMPIAN INFIDELITY

There was a time when Zeus became enamored of Io, a princess of Argos. Patiently, he waited for a moment when Hera's hawklike eyes would stray. When the opportunity finally presented itself, he flew down to Io's bedchamber, where he seduced her by whispering sweet nothings in her ears while she slept, thus convincing her to let him inside her dreams, where he would make love to her.

While Zeus normally planned ways to conceal his affairs from Hera, it was not until late in the act that he realized that Hera might see this infidelity. Zeus quickly wrapped the earth in a blanket of dark clouds, hoping to hide his adultery. Hera, however, immediately saw through this feeble deception and flew down to earth, her eyes blazing with anger. But instead of catching Zeus in the act, she came across her husband standing calmly next to a white heifer. When she asked him what he was doing standing next to a cow, he replied that he'd been standing there when the cow had suddenly sprung from the earth.

Hera, however, was not to be fooled; she knew the cow must be the illicit lover, transformed by her husband at the last possible moment. No matter how hard Hera pressed, Zeus stuck to his story. In order to catch her husband in his lie, Hera asked Argus, a hundred-eyed herdsman, to watch over the supposed heifer. She was sure Zeus would turn the cow back into a human the next time he desired her, and when he did, Argus would alert Hera to the indiscretion.

Not to be bested, Zeus sent Hermes, the god of trickery, to slay the watchman. This was no easy task since Argus never closed all of his one hundred eyes at the same time. But the god of thieves had a plan. He pretended to be a simple country fellow who was adept at playing the pipes and telling stories. Hermes interested Argus in his melodic tales, and soon the monster was captivated by the yarns, yet not enough to take his eyes off Io. Hermes gradually told duller stories and played less melodic music until he told a story so dull and played music so boring that Argus fell asleep. The second all one hundred eyes were closed, Hermes quickly killed the herdsman. (Feeling it a shame to waste Argus' odd appearance, Hermes quickly placed all one hundred eyes in the tail of the peacock.)

Although Io was now free of Argus, Hera had been expecting this. She ordered a gadfly to torment and bite Io, who was still in cow form. The merciless little fly did its job well, sending Io into such fits of pain that she eventually tried to rid herself of the torturous little insect by running great distances and swimming great oceans. The Ionian Sea and the Bosphorus Strait, meaning "channel of the cow," are both named after her. Eventually she ran to Egypt, to the banks of the Nile, where the fly lost interest in her and flew away. Zeus then transformed her back into the lovely woman she had been.

By this time Hera figured that Io had been killed during her insane frenzy, and she forgot about her. Zeus used this to his advantage and quickly made love to Io once again, this time conceiving with her a son, Ephastus, a forefather of the mighty Heracles.

Bust of Jupiter, Roman copy after Greek original.

POSEIDON—GOD
OF THE OCEANS

The son of Kronos and the brother of Zeus and Hades, Poseidon (or Neptune, as he was called by the Romans) was the god of the oceans. He ruled the waves as completely as Zeus ruled the heavens and Hades ruled the land of the dead. The three-pronged trident was his symbol—the equivalent of Zeus' thunderbolts—and it signified his control over the seas and both the beneficent (as when it was used to spear fish) and malevolent (as when it was used against man) natures of the world's waters.

Head of bronze figure, c. 460 B.C. The identity of this figure—whether he is meant to be Zeus or Poseidon—is still a matter of debate among classical scholars.

gle glance, he fathered the Giant Chrysaor. The Cyclops Polyphemus, who caused so much trouble for Odysseus on his return from Troy, was also a son of the sea god. Two of his other sons, Otus and Ephialtes, known collectively as the Aloidae, imprisoned Ares, the god of war, in a bronze cask for thirteen months and pursued Artemis and Hera, intent on rape. (They were defeated by the gods and given eternal punishment in Tartarus.) In fact, so many of Poseidon's children invoked the wrath of both god and man, either for their physical ugliness or the ugliness of their deeds, that Poseidon soon found it easier to bury his vile offspring under the earth than to watch over them and make sure they kept out of trouble.

Besides being god of the seas, Poseidon was also the god of both horses and earthquakes. He was believed to have been the god that first gave the tamed horse to man to be used to plow fields, to carry heavy loads, and as transportation. The ancient Greeks believed that the manes of Poseidon's aquatic steeds could be seen in the waves of the sea.

The earthquake was also attributed to Poseidon. In *The Iliad*, Homer often refers to Poseidon as the "Shaker of the Earth," a title he richly deserved.

When the reign of the Olympians was young, each of the gods selected earthly regions that would be sacred specifically to him or her alone. Naturally, some arguments arose

ABOVE: *Polyphemus the Cyclops*, Giulio Romano, 1525–1535. A son of Poseidon, Polyphemus was outwitted in his own home by the always clever Odysseus.

RIGHT: Poseidon reprimands his son Ephialtes for crimes against the gods.

Poseidon took for his wife the Nereid, or water nymph, Amphitrite. Like his younger brother Zeus, however, Poseidon possessed a voracious sexual appetite and was often unfaithful. But whereas Zeus seemed to have an eye for the lovely and beguiling, Poseidon seemed indifferent to the physical characteristics of his concubines. This indifference occasionally resulted in his offspring being some of the vilest and most terrifying creatures in the classical canon.

By the Gorgon Medusa, a terrifying creature with snakes for hair and the ability to turn men to stone with a sin-

when several gods desired reign over the same area. Poseidon always ended up getting the worst of the deal. In the end, all he could lay claim to was the legendary island of Atlantis, which according to some stories, eventually lost favor in his eyes. He brought upon the island an earthquake of such magnitude that Atlantis was literally torn apart, disappearing forever into the depths of the sea.

Along with his brothers Zeus and Hades and his sister Demeter, the goddess of vegetation, Poseidon was one of the four chthonic gods, that is, those deities who had control over the powerful forces of nature. To the ancient Greeks, the oceans were a limitless source of wonder. Why is the sea covered with waves, they wondered. Why do the waters sometimes turn destructive, ruining crops and flooding and eroding the coastline? How can something that supplies a man with food also be able to quickly kill the same man if he falls out of his boat?

To this day, the ocean continues to be an extremely powerful force over which humans have little control. It is doubtful that we will ever be able to understand the seas or to bring them under our control. The oceans of the world seem petulant, responding to whatever whim takes them, and capable of terrible vindictiveness and violence, as in the case of hurricanes and coastal storms.

Such a character fits Poseidon perfectly. Just as when man is dealing with the sea, caution should be exercised at all times when dealing with the god of the oceans—all it takes is one slip or mistake and the waters will be one's doom.

— Conclusion

LEFT: Mosaic of Neptune from Palermo, Italy, c. A.D. 1st century.

BELOW: Although Poseidon was known primarily as the ruler of the oceans, he was also the god of horses.

HADES
AND DEMETER

HADES—KING OF THE DEAD

The brother of Zeus and Poseidon, Hades (or Pluto as the Romans referred to him) was the lord of the underworld and the god of wealth. He is often perceived as an evil god simply because he rules over a particularly unpleasant realm. Occasionally, he is even mistaken for Death himself. Neither of these characterizations is correct. Hades is not the god of death. That role belongs to Thanatos, who, with his brother Sleep, resides in Hades'

**Relief of the face of Hades from a Greek
krater, 4th century B.C.**

31

kingdom. Hades is not an evil god; he simply has a rather unpleasant job that by association colors his reputation.

Hades was always a just and fair god. He had a strict set of rules by which he governed the underworld, and he rarely—and then usually only against his will—broke those rules. He is generally portrayed as a god with a dark visage who is cloaked in shadows and rarely, if ever, shows himself. During the war with the Titans, the Cyclopes fashioned for him a magical helmet that rendered him invisible. He wore this helmet whenever he ventured forth from his shadowy realm.

Of all the gods, Hades alone was not welcome on Mount Olympus. It may be that the Olympians, all of whom possessed human prejudices and character flaws, were as put off by Hades as were the mortals who feared him.

GEOGRAPHY
OF THE
UNDERWORLD

In many Homeric and pre-Homeric Greek myths, Hades' kingdom is described simply as a shadowy realm where spirits wander aimlessly back and forth, bemoaning the fact that their lives are over. It was the Roman imagination that created a distinct geography for his dark world.

The underworld as imagined by the Romans consisted of four separate regions. Tartarus, the area that most people would consider "hell," was the blackest and most vile of the four, the place where those mortals who had committed evil during their lives were sent for all eternity. Like the Christian hell, Tartarus was the place of eternal punishment.

The opposite of Tartarus, the "heaven" of the underworld, was Elysium (which is some-

times referred to as the Elysian Fields). Ruled by the dethroned Kronos, this region was an area of light and perpetual day, a realm of eternal happiness where music played continuously and good cheer was always in the air. The inhabitants of Elysium, those souls who had led honest and virtuous lives, were able to wish themselves back to life whenever they grew weary of the afterlife.

The third area of Hades was the Asphodel Fields, so named for the Asphodel, the pale flowers that blanketed the mournful ground. This was where most departed souls resided.

The fourth area of the underworld was Erebus, and this was where Hades' palace was located. Occasionally, Erebus was depicted as the first area the dead must pass through on their way to the underworld.

The underworld was also home to five rivers, all of which have specific symbolic functions. The Acheron and the Styx often served the same function, and hence often were interchangeable. These were the first rivers the newly dead had to cross. The Styx was considered so holy that an oath sworn by it could never be broken, not even by Zeus himself. Upon reaching the underworld, the

RIGHT: Marble relief from a Roman sarcophagus, c. A.D. 1st–2nd century, showing Charon, the ferryman of the river Styx, demanding payment from recently dead souls before transporting them to the gates of the underworld.

BELOW: Hades upon his throne in Erebus. Cerberus, the three-headed watchdog of the underworld's gates, stands faithfully at his side.

newly dead would wait on the shore of the Styx until Charon, the ferryman, appeared. The ancient Greek custom of burying loved ones with a small coin in their mouths was the result of the Greek belief that Charon required payment in return for safe passage to the gates of Hades. Without payment, Charon would refuse his service and the dead would be stranded for all time on the banks of the Styx, forever denied their eternal rest.

Three other rivers also lay inside Hades' gates. The river Cocytus was the river of la-

mentation; it was by drinking the waters of this river that souls fully realized the wonder of life and came to understand all that they had lost by dying. The river Phlegethon was the river of fire; its services were put to use mainly in Tartarus, where its painful, undying flames were used to torture the evil. The river Lethe provided the most merciful service of all five Hadean rivers; once the spirits of the dead drank from its waters, they would blissfully forget their past lives and become content with their new existence.

After being ferried across the Styx (or the Acheron) by Charon, the dead arrived at the gates to Hades, which were guarded by Cerberus, a three-headed demon watchdog with the tail of a serpent. His job, which he performed with unerring fidelity, was simple: to make sure that every soul that went in never came back out again.

Once inside, the dead were faced with judgment. There was a trio of judges who heard and reviewed each spirit's life story, then determined whether the soul deserved to go to Tartarus, Elysium, or the Asphodel Fields. The first of these judges was Aeacus, who in life had been a kind, fair, and pious king of Aegina. The second judge was King Minos, who had ruled the island of Crete with a fair and just hand. Rhadamanthys, the brother of Minos, was the last of the three. Although he had never been a king, he had a sense of justice noble enough to earn him a position as judge of the dead. All three were mortal sons of Zeus.

According to some myths, the Erinnyes, or the Furies, as they were sometimes called, also inhabited the underworld, forever torturing murderers and those individuals who had directly or indirectly shed the blood of their own kind.

DEMETER— GODDESS OF VEGETATION

The daughter of Kronos and Rhea and the sister of Zeus, Poseidon, and Hades, Demeter was one of the original Olympians. She was the goddess of the earth's vegetation—its plants, flowers, and grains. She is paired with Hades in this chapter because the most prominent myth concerning her also involves Hades.

THE MYTH OF PERSEPHONE

Demeter had a single daughter, Persephone, by her brother Zeus. Hades took notice of the young goddess one day while she was lying in a field admiring a flower. He fell in love with her at first sight. Using his godly powers, Hades caused the earth near Persephone to split open. He flew out, grabbed the surprised Persephone, and dragged her down into the depths of his murky kingdom.

Roman statue of Ceres, the goddess of vegetation and the mother of Proserpïna, c. A.D. 420. Ceres was the Roman name for Demeter; Proserpïna was what the Romans called Persephone.

The Rape of Proserpïna, Niccolo dell'Abate, 16th century.

When Persephone failed to return from her afternoon stroll, Demeter became extremely worried and set out to find her. After a long search, she discovered what had happened, who had taken her daughter, and why. Enraged, she swore that the earth would not receive the gifts she usually bestowed upon it until her daughter was returned—it would become a barren, dead world without flower, tree, or field of grain.

She renounced her seat on Olympus and exiled herself to the earth, angered that her fellow gods did nothing to aid her. Roaming the earth as an old woman, Demeter came to the kingdom of Eleusis, where she was be-

friended by a kind woman named Metaneira. In return for the woman's hospitality, Demeter bestowed upon Demophoön, the woman's infant son, the innate knowledge of growing and harvesting corn, which, when the boy grew to manhood, would prove invaluable to the whole of humanity. Still Demeter refused to return to the earth its bounty. With every day that passed, the earth grew more desolate.

After a time, Zeus decided that this had to stop. He asked each of the Olympians to try to convince Demeter to lift her curse. The gods pleaded with her, but Demeter's outrage and sorrow were too great and she refused even to listen to her fellow gods. Having no other option, Zeus knew he must either convince Hades to let Persephone leave the underworld to see her mother or resolve himself to reigning over a barren husk of a world.

Hades couldn't refuse his brother, so he granted Persephone a temporary freedom. Before she left, he tricked her into eating three seeds from a pomegranate, a traditional symbol of fertility and marital obligations. As a result, Persephone was bound to return to him every year. It was soon decided that Persephone would stay with her mother on Mount Olympus for nine months out of every year—spring through autumn, the growing season. As soon as harvesting had begun across the earth, she would return to Hades and rule as queen of the underworld. During this time nothing would grow on the earth.

In the myth of Persephone we see an interesting interaction between the forces of life and growth and the forces of death. We are presented with an example of how ancient man characterized the cyclical aspect of nature. It is stories like this one that make the study of myth much more than simply the investigation of tales of gods and heroes.

Greek vase, c. 330 B.C., showing Hades and his wife, Persephone, at their palace in the underworld. Since Persephone is with her husband, it must be winter on the earth.

APHRODITE
AND ARES

APHRODITE—GODDESS OF
ROMANTIC AND SEXUAL LOVE

Aphrodite (or Venus, as the Romans called her) was the goddess of both sexual and romantic love. The Greek personification of physical beauty, she represented both raw lust and gentle affection, and it was she who caused young, single people to fall in love and older, married folks to commit adultery.

The Birth of Venus, Eugene Amaury-Duval,
19th century.

Physically, Aphrodite was the most beautiful of all the Olympians. There are two different stories concerning Aphrodite's birth. In *The Iliad* she is the daughter of Zeus and the Titaness Dione. The majority of post-Homeric poets, however, tell how the goddess was born from the combination of the sea and Uranus' castrated genitalia. After Kronos hurled his father's privates into the sea, the waves swirled around them, creating a mass of foam that became the goddess.

If Aphrodite were created as recounted in the latter version, she would be older than the rest of the Olympians. This is somehow more sensible than Homer's version, since without the qualities and temperaments Aphrodite instills in others, Kronos and Rhea may not have had six children. Maybe they wouldn't have had any children. Maybe they would have grown bored with each other and not had Zeus. Of course, this speculation is all in fun, but it makes sense that the goddess of sexual love and desire should predate the core Olympians.

The philosopher Plato reconciled the issue by saying that there were in fact two goddesses of love. The one born of the sea foam he called Urania. She was the goddess of romantic, pure love. The other, the daughter of Zeus and Dione, he dubbed Pandemos. She represented the base, earthly sexual desires. But Plato came up with that idea long after many of the Greek religious beliefs were cemented in the culture. And in those myths, there was one goddess of love, both sexual and romantic, the epitome of physical beauty, who was incredibly jealous of competition and vindictive when opposed.

Aphrodite is usually said to be the wife of Hephaestus, the god of fire and blacksmiths, and the mother of the Eros of the later myths, the cherubic archer whose arrows are love.

Red-figured skyphos, c. 420–410 B.C., showing Aphrodite and her son Eros. It is unclear whether the child's father was Ares or Hermes, and it is doubtful whether Aphrodite herself knew which god was the true father.

Some of Aphrodite's children bore the unmistakable stigma of bizarre genital aberration. After seducing Hermes, Aphrodite gave birth to Hermaphroditus, a being with both male and female genitalia. Her union with Dionysus, the god of wine, resulted in the birth of Priapus, an ugly but talented child who would go on to become a woodland deity, famous for both his skills in gardening and his elephantine phallus.

Although she was married, Aphrodite never held her vows of fidelity too close to her heart. She was, after all, the goddess of lust, and unbridled desire seldom abides by the rules of marriage. One of her favorite and most powerful lovers was Ares, the god of war, with whom she conceived three children. This relationship is interesting in that the other gods never cared a great deal for Ares.

ARES—GOD
OF WAR

The son of Zeus and Hera (and perhaps Zeus' only legitimate son), Ares was a thick-headed, temperamental, violent god. Since he, like Aphrodite, is the personification of one of man's base qualities, it is only fitting that his actions and attitudes should betray a rather primitive and thoughtless mentality.

Ares loved battle for its own sake. He rarely cared for the reason behind war; his passion was the shriek of metal on metal, sweat and dust, the bloodlust of battle, the thrill of victory. This shallow attitude made him quite unpopular on Olympus. The only gods who cared for him were Aphrodite; Hades, who was always happy to receive new

souls; and his sister Eris, the goddess of discord. The other Olympians found him to be a bore because all he did was swagger around Olympus talking about battle. Like their gods, the Greeks wanted little to do with Ares. They recognized but did not respect the god of war. They realized there was a bit of Ares in all of them but were rather ashamed of that fact. This being the case, Ares never figured prominently in the Greek canon.

It was the Romans who gave Mars (the Roman name for Ares) the character he is famous for, that of a brave, cunning, and brilliant warlord. This makes sense when one considers the different cultural mindsets of Greece and Rome. The Greeks, though they had large, well-trained armies, were generally more concerned with peaceful endeavors such as philosophy and the arts, while the Romans concerned themselves more with waging war and expanding an empire.

CAUGHT
IN THE ACT

Ares and Aphrodite were rather careless when it came to their liaisons—it was no secret to any of the Olympians that they were romantically involved.

During one of their trysts, Helios, the driver of the sun-chariot, spied the two in bed as he began his ascent across the morning sky. He immediately sent word to Hephaestus, who devised a plan to catch the lovers in the act. After fashioning a net of bronze, which he hammered so thin as to be invisible, the god of blacksmiths crept into Aphrodite's bed-

While it is generally said that Hermaphroditus was the result of a union between Hermes and Aphrodite, in an alternate myth concerning Hermaphroditus' origin, the double-sexed being is the result of the nymph of the Carian fountain praying to be united with a male named Hermaphroditus.

Roman statue of Mars,
Hellenistic period.
The Romans, being
extremely fond of the
god of war, created
many artworks
honoring him, while
the Greeks rarely
depicted him.

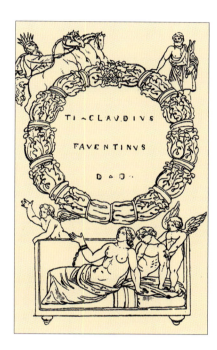

chamber while the illicit lovers were away and affixed the corners of the net to the four posts of the bed, then went to Aphrodite and told her that, as he needed a holiday, he would be going away for a while.

As soon as Hephaestus was out the door, Aphrodite quickly called on Ares, informing him that as long as her husband was away, the palace would be theirs. The god of war soon arrived and the lovers fell on the bed, where their smiles and laughs quickly changed to curses and vain struggles—Hephaestus' net was too strong, even in the face of the mighty god of war. In order to embarrass and discredit the two adulterers, Hephaestus, who had not left at all, called all the Olympians to gather as witnesses and judges.

The goddesses, out of modesty, refused to set eyes on the spectacle, but the male gods all huddled around the bed, nudging and winking at each other. Hermes even ventured to say that he wouldn't mind being in Ares' predicament even with three nets and the goddesses looking on. This crassness met with a good-natured round of laughter from all. Shamed and disgraced, Ares and Aphrodite fled to different parts of the earth to lie low for a while and allow everyone to cool down.

APOLLO AND ARTEMIS— THE TWINS OF JUSTICE

THE BIRTH OF THE TWINS

After an affair with Zeus, the Titaness Leto was forced to wander the earth in an effort to escape the wrath of the jealous Hera. The queen of the gods sent the monstrous Python, a large and vicious serpent, to hunt Leto, thinking that as the object of Python's hunt, Leto would never have time to rest or be safe long enough to deliver her children. The Titaness seemed doomed to wander the earth forever, but Poseidon soon took pity on her

Terra-cotta plaque, Hellenistic period, from the Temple of Apollo on the Palatine in Rome depicting Apollo and Diana decorating a sacred pillar.

and granted her sanctuary on the island of Delos. Here, Leto finally gave birth to Apollo and Artemis.

APOLLO— GOD OF LIGHT AND TRUTH

Apollo, the younger of the twins, represented everything that the Greeks themselves strove for; he was *the* male archetype. As Aphrodite was the epitome of female beauty, Apollo was the paragon of male beauty. His clarity and stability of mind were the greatest of any member of the pantheon. His talents in the artistic and medicinal fields were unmatched by god or man.

Also, it was believed that it went against Apollo's grain to lie, that he was in fact incapable of falsehood or misrepresentation. As a result, Apollo's oracles were by far the most trusted in all of Greece. The most famous of these was the Oracle at Delphi on the island of Delos, said to be near the area where Apollo slew Python a mere four days after being born. This particular temple of Apollo grew in renown until it was famous throughout the ancient world. Pilgrimages to Apollo's Oracle at Delphi were made from the farthest reaches of Greece and beyond to pay tribute to the god of light and to ask Pythia, his priestess, for guidance.

Another of Apollo's godly aspects was his complete knowledge of all evil existing in the world. He could see and hear any malicious act, and he knew how such an act could be stopped. It is for this reason that his oracle was consulted not only on such questions as land disputes and personal problems, but also about such calamities as plague and disease.

Typical of the gods, Apollo was insanely jealous of anyone questioning or challenging his talents. It was in situations like this that the violent side of the god emerged, a lesson to man that no matter how advanced one becomes, it is always possible to fall back into the old primitive, violent ways.

THE MYTH OF MARSYAS

One day Athena, the goddess of invention, constructed a flute. At first, she was pleased with her creation because it made such beautiful sounds. But when she realized that her cheeks puffed out when she played, distorting her otherwise perfect face, she threw the instrument aside.

A Satyr (a woodland spirit of virility) named Marsyas came across the discarded flute, picked it up, and began to play. After some time he became so proficient in his playing that he believed himself to be the finest musician ever, better even than Apollo. He was so certain of his talents that he challenged the god to a musical contest. The nine Muses, the spirits of artistic endeavors, were to be the judges. Apollo, calmly cradling his lyre, waited for Marsyas to finish his songs, which, although very good, couldn't compare to the music Apollo could make. The Muses were overcome by their lord's playing. Apollo was deemed the winner, and in retribution for having challenged him in the first place, he strung Marsyas to a tree and skinned him alive, the Satyr's screams now filling the woods with a much more sinister music.

Diana of Versailles,
Leochares,
4th century B.C.,
Roman copy after
Greek statue. Diana
was the Roman name
for Artemis.

ARTEMIS—
GODDESS
OF THE HUNT

Artemis became aware of her new duties as a goddess mere seconds after she was born—immediately after Leto delivered her, the newborn Artemis helped deliver her brother Apollo, and from that point on, Artemis was the goddess of childbirth and the protector of children. This, however, is generally considered a secondary aspect, for Artemis is most well known as the goddess of the hunt.

Tall in stature and strong of build, Artemis would have proved a match for any of the male gods. Without peer as a hunter and Ares' equal as a warrior, Artemis nonetheless possessed enough physical beauty to make even Aphrodite jealous. Unlike the goddess of love, however, Artemis was forever chaste. In fact, Aphrodite's promiscuousness infuriated Artemis; she found it very distasteful that marriage vows could be so easily forgotten. Because of this, she avenged the victims of infidelity whenever she could. She also considered rape, especially the rape of virgins, to be an inexcusable crime. When she learned of a rape, she would immediately punish the rapist, showing him not the slightest bit of mercy.

While Apollo was the god of truth and prophecy, Artemis was the goddess of human rights. It was she

who stood up for the quiet and just, the meek and unthreatening, the defiled virgins, the underdogs. Together, these two illustrate the classical conception of justice.

THE MYTH OF ACTAEON

On occasion, Artemis' steadfastness in her beliefs caused undue pain and suffering and served as a reminder to man that any cause, if taken to extremes, can prove to be just as unjust and damaging as the evil it purports to fight against.

While hunting in the woods with his faithful pack of hunting dogs one day, the great hunter Actaeon accidentally came across the naked Artemis bathing in a woodland pond. Since she was a goddess, possessing a beauty never before dreamed of in his mortal mind, his human curiosity led him to hide in the bushes and stare in wonderment and admiration.

A gentle snap of a twig alerted Artemis to his presence. Her first reaction was to let him go since he'd come across her purely by accident. But she realized that to let him go would only lead to trouble—soon he would be back home, drinking with his friends, and would brag about having seen the "virgin goddess" naked. Artemis, who had sworn a vow of chastity and had vowed that no one would ever see her naked, could not allow this mortal to remain at large. She transformed the poor hunter into a stag of such noble and grand stature that his hunting dogs immediately fell upon him, having no idea that it was actually their master they were tearing limb from limb, his blood on their muzzles.

Diana and Actaeon, Cavalier d'Arpino, late 16th–mid 17th century.

ATHENA AND HEPHAESTUS—ARCHITECTS OF CIVILIZATION

ATHENA—GODDESS OF INVENTION

Of all the births in the Greek pantheon, Athena's is one of the oddest. She was not born of a female, but from the head of her father, Zeus. Her mother was Metis, whom Zeus swallowed when he learned she was pregnant with his child. Soon after this terrible deed, the king of the gods experienced a great deal of pain, which for a long time he thought was simply a massive headache. The pain grew and grew, and eventually, out of desperation,

---

Minerva (the Roman version of Athena),
head for Lemnian statue, Hellenistic period,
Roman copy after Phidias.

51

Zeus asked Hephaestus to take his hammer and bash open Zeus' head. When Hephaestus split Zeus' skull, Athena leapt out, fully grown and fully armed.

The goddess of wisdom and invention, Athena was credited with creating such tools as the bridle, the yoke, the plow, and the rake. She also created the flute and the trumpet, as well as mathematics. The clay pot and the skills of homemaking also came from Athena. She gave man not only the essentials for making a home but also the tools and ideas for creating a civilization. All this considered, it comes as no surprise that Athens, one of the most advanced cities of the ancient world, was considered her home city.

In the minds of the early Greeks, Athena was not as peace-loving as her generosity may imply. Homer described her as a rather war-like goddess, and she was in fact considered to be the goddess of war, the female counterpart of Ares. For her, however, war was not blind, unplanned battle, as it was for Ares, but strategic and ordered combat.

LEFT: As the rest of the Olympians look on, Athena leaps out of her father's head.

BELOW: Hephaestus, the god of metallurgy, was lamed after Hera threw him off Mount Olympus in disgust at his ugliness and deformities.

BELOW LEFT: Hephaestus informs Athena of his desire for her, but the goddess of invention stands aloof. This desire eventually overcame Hephaestus and he attempted to rape the goddess.

During the Trojan War, Athena sided with the Greek army. It was while under her influence that the mortal hero Diomedes successfully attacked and wounded Ares, who then complained about his half-sister to an inattentive Zeus. This situation points out a major difference between the two deities of war—Athena was level-headed and intelligent; Ares was, both intellectually and emotionally, a child.

Like Artemis, Athena was a chaste goddess, but for different, less prudish reasons—she simply found the advances of the male gods infantile and silly. She was attracted to none of them, and therefore did not desire their affections. Unfortunately, the disinterest was not mutual; she was constantly being hounded by the other gods, and countered their flirtations with silence and their advances with swift, brutal kicks in tender areas.

HEPHAESTUS— GOD OF SMITHS AND METALLURGY

Hephaestus was the god of craftsmanship, the deity of those who worked with fire. He was the god of blacksmiths and artisans. He was married to Aphrodite, but he rarely received her affections.

There are two versions of the story of Hephaestus' birth. According to one, he was the son of Zeus and Hera; in the other, he was the son of Hera, who had conceived him alone in an attempt to spite Zeus for Athena's parthenogenetic birth. In both versions, when Hera saw what she had given birth to—Hephaestus was both ugly and deformed—she hurled the infant from the heights of Mount Olympus. He landed in the ocean and was immediately rescued by the nymphs Thetis and Eurynome, who raised the god and encouraged his interest in blacksmithing, providing him with a suitable smithy where he created not only weapons and armor but also beautiful pieces of jewelry.

Hera once visited Thetis on a social call and complimented her on a lovely jeweled pin she was wearing. She asked Thetis where she had acquired such a beautiful object, but Thetis was reluctant to answer, as she did not want to let Hera know that her deformed son was still alive for fear she might again try to murder him. Eventually, Hera dragged the truth from Thetis and took her son back to Olympus, where she provided him with the finest forge imaginable.

Hephaestus was very happy that his mother had finally accepted him, and when Zeus punished Hera by hanging her from her wrists after discovering her role in one of the

Greek statue of
Athena and
Erichthonius (nestled
at her bosom), copy
after Cephisodotus,
4th century B.C.

many attempted coups against him, Hephaestus became very angry. He approached the king of the heavens and condemned him for his actions. Disgruntled, Zeus threw the god of blacksmiths from the heights of Olympus, and this time Hephaestus landed on the island of Lemnos. The impact broke both of Hephaestus' legs and from that point on he was permanently lame, able to walk around Olympus only with the support of crutches or, in some mythological accounts, golden leg braces of his own design.

While Athena provided man with sophisticated instruments, Hephaestus supplied the basic, rudimentary tools. It was Hephaestus who created the plow blade, the sword, the spearhead, and other such implements. Together these two gods gave man the tools needed for civilization to take root; without their gifts, it would have taken man much longer to stop living nomadically and to settle down into cities and towns.

THE RAPE OF
ATHENA

It was no secret that Athena considered herself "unattainable," and this attitude often prompted cruel and malicious acts on the part of her fellow Olympians.

Once, when Athena was planning to go and see her half-brother Hephaestus to ask him to make her some armor, Poseidon told the smith that she was on her way with lust

on her mind and expected to be made love to. When she arrived at the smithy and requested the arms, Hephaestus would not allow her to pay him, stating instead that he would do the job for love. Thinking this to mean that the god would do the work for free, with her gratitude his only compensation, Athena agreed and watched the god work his wonders, toiling away at a magnificent set of arms. When he was finished he threw himself upon her, his mind racing with lust. Athena threw him off herself, but not before he deposited some of his semen on her thigh. Outraged at such a violation, Athena wiped the semen off her leg and flung it down to the earth, which then became pregnant with Hephaestus' child. Gaea was revolted at the thought of giving birth to a child of Hephaestus and refused to be held at all responsible for the child's welfare.

Because of her kind nature, Athena could not just let the child perish. She assumed responsibility for the infant, whom she named Erichthonius. The child was hideous, not simply deformed like his father but a new sort of creature—half-serpent, half-human. Eventually, this man-snake would become the first king of Athens, teaching his subjects to revere and worship his adopted mother. In another version of this myth, Hephaestus' semen falls onto a snow-covered mountainside, from which the first statues sprout. Metaphorically, this version is much more satisfying, since it makes sense that the union of wisdom and handicrafts, whether or not it was fully successful, should produce art.

Black-figured amphora, 6th century B.C., depicting Athena standing between two columns on which cocks are perched. This amphora was given as a prize for a footrace winner at the Panathenaic Games.

HERMES
AND DIONYSUS

HERMES—GOD OF THIEVES,
COMMERCE, AND CUNNING

S on of Zeus and the nymph Maia, daughter of the Titan Atlas, Hermes earned

his reputation as a trickster early on. Soon after his birth in a cave on Mount

Cyllene, Maia, satisfied that her newborn was healthy, turned her back on

him for a few minutes in order to freshen up and regain her composure. In

the short time that her back was turned, the young Hermes sprouted into

Mercury, Tiepolo Giambattista, 18th century.
Mercury was the Roman version of Hermes.

boyhood and sneaked away from the cave to explore the surrounding countryside.

He soon came across Apollo tending a herd of cattle, which the young god immediately decided to steal as a prank. He waited until Apollo was asleep, and to make sure he covered his tracks, as well as those of the cows, he led the cattle off the field backward, making them walk in their own hoofprints so that no fresh ones would be made. Once he was out of sight he fashioned shoes for the cattle that would make no impressions on the soft earth. He then led the herd back to the cave of his birth, feeling quite successful in his first escapade.

When Apollo discovered that his cattle were missing, he enlisted the aid of the Satyrs, the forest spirits who were the personifications of unbridled nature, to find them. The wood spirits searched the forest from end to end, leaving no path or clue unchecked. Eventually, one of the scouting parties came across the cave on Mount Cyllene, hearing enchant-

ing music coming from its mouth. As they approached, Hermes' nurse emerged from the cave and told them that the music was being made by the young god. The divine child, she told them, had constructed a wonderful musical instrument from the shell of a tortoise, using fresh cowgut as strings. The Satyrs immediately returned to Apollo and told him what they had discovered. Apollo went to the cave, seized the young Hermes, and brought him to Olympus to answer to Zeus for the obvious crime.

Zeus didn't want to find his young son guilty but, after hearing the evidence, he found he had no choice. When Hermes realized that his father didn't believe his lies, he confessed to the theft and promised to return the majority of Apollo's herd. He couldn't return all the animals, he said, because he'd already killed two of the cows, used their guts for his lyre's strings, and divided the succulent meat into equal portions that he'd offered to the gods in sacrifice.

Zeus then examined the slaughtered cows and noticed that there was one sacrificial portion too many. When he asked Hermes about this miscalculation, the young god responded that he had apportioned one sacrificial lot for himself. Zeus couldn't help but smile inwardly at this boldness. In order to clear the air between himself and his half-brother, Hermes offered Apollo not only the return of his herd but the lyre as well. Intrigued by the new instrument, Apollo agreed; soon, after Apollo had practiced with it for a while, the lyre became Apollo's signature instrument.

Zeus was so impressed by the ingenuity and resourcefulness of his young son that he bestowed upon him many duties and honors, all worthy of his crafty nature. Although Zeus knew that Hermes would try to tell the truth whenever he was asked a question, he realized that his son would not always tell the entire truth if it was not in his best interests. Because of this, Hermes became the god of business and commerce.

Hermes soon found that his new duties weren't limited merely to business. Because of his cunning, he also became the god of rhetoric and the misleading sentence. His sphere of influence was soon extended to include lovers, coworkers, and government officials. Because of his stealth and quickness of foot, Hermes became the messenger of the gods; he was dispatched whenever one god needed to speak to another over great distances. He was also the guide of the dead. Only Hermes knew the path leading to the underworld, and it was he who led the recently departed souls down to Hades' dark domain.

Since he was the errand-boy of the gods, knowledgeable of all roads and pathways on heaven and earth, Hermes became the patron god of travelers. At major crossroads through-out ancient Greece rectangular pillars topped with the bearded face of Hermes were erected. If a traveler approached a fork and found himself confused as to which way to go, he would put his faith in Hermes to guide him down the correct path.

Hermes' occupation as messenger of the gods ensured that he figured prominently in many myths, more so than almost any other god except for Zeus.

DIONYSUS— GOD OF INTOXICATION

Dionysus was the only Olympian whose mother was mortal. He is also the only Olympian to be "born" three times.

Stamnos, c. 4th–3rd century B.C., depicting Dionysus presiding over a ritual ceremony performed by the Maenads, his frenzied and ecstatic followers.

Greek vasepainting,
c. 4th century B.C.,
depicting Dionysus
and his mother,
Semele.

One of the many mortals desired by Zeus was a beautiful princess of Thebes named Semele. The king of the heavens courted her time and again, finally swearing by the river Styx that he would do whatever she asked of him. When Hera learned of her husband's newest infatuation, she immediately began to scheme against him. She planted in Semele's head the desire to see Zeus as he truly was, not in the guise of a mortal.

When Semele told Zeus of this desire, he tried very hard to change her mind, but to no avail. With a heavy heart, the king of the gods revealed his true form to her and she fell down dead. Zeus removed the unborn Dionysus from her womb and placed him in his thigh, where he continued to grow until he was born. When the child was fully grown, he emerged from Zeus' thigh.

As soon as the young Dionysus was born, Hera ordered a group of Titans to lure him away from his father's protective gaze with wondrous presents and toys. The lures proved too tempting to the young god, and as soon

as he was out of range of his father's watchful eye, the Titans grabbed him, tore him limb from limb, and roasted and ate his flesh.

Athena, however, found and saved the child's heart, and Zeus was able to salvage his limbs. They buried the remains, and Rhea, recombining the pieces, brought the child back to life. This was the first time the god experienced the cycle of death and resurrection, a cycle he would repeat again and again, just as the grapevine dies every winter and is born again in the spring.

Zeus now placed his bastard son in the care of Athamas, king of Orchomenos, and his concubine, Semele's sister, Ino. On the advice of Hermes, the two mortals disguised the young Dionysus in girl's clothes, hoping to trick Hera, who was not in the slightest deceived. In retaliation, she caused Athamas to fly into an insane rage and kill his son Learchus. With the blood of his child not yet cold on his hands, the king turned his murderous attention to Ino. As he advanced, Dionysus blinded him so that instead of killing

his lover he slaughtered a goat. Filled with grief, Ino threw herself into the sea soon after. Zeus, remembering her kindness toward the young god of wine, decided that she would not be sent to Hades; instead, he transformed her into the sea goddess Leucothea. At the same time, Dionysus was transformed by Zeus into a young goat, and then entrusted to a group of oreads (mountain nymphs) living on Mount Nysa. It was here that Dionysus learned of the grape and, through experimentation, created wine.

Dionysus, more than any other god, personifies the extremes of human nature. As the god of intoxication, he is the god of both the insane, drunken rage and the introspective, drunken calm—he is at once man's destroyer and his benefactor. The god of wine appears in many myths, and is often a stock character in stories that involve drunkenness. He is also the personification of the cyclical pattern of nature. Like the grapevine, Dionysus was said to die every year, only to be reborn when the first new shoot appeared in the spring.

THE
LESSER OLYMPIANS

While it is the major Olympians who flavor classical mythology with their strong personalities (and who are at the center or on the sidelines of most Greek myths), there is a second tier of gods that supply the canon with the subtle colorings that are related more to purely human nature. These lesser gods were never called upon for help by heroes in crisis and never figured prominently in any myths; they were the gods and goddesses of everyday life.

The Muse Calliope, Eustache Le Sueur, c. 1650. Though Calliope was generally portrayed holding a scroll or stylus, the artist chose to paint her playing the harp.

HESTIA— GODDESS OF THE HEARTH

Hestia was one of Zeus' sisters. Although she was one of the original Olympians, along with Hera, Poseidon, Demeter, Hades, and Zeus, her duties in the pantheon relegated her to a role that was lacking in drama. Hestia was the goddess of hearth and home, the deity who kept watch over the homestead, making sure that no harm came to the family. She had no discernible personality and never played an essential role in any major myths. She was quite simply the "home goddess." Like the hearth itself, she was content to serve those who drew warmth and comfort from her.

The Temple of the Vestal Virgins in ancient Rome was dedicated to the goddess Vesta (the Roman name for Hestia). Inside this temple, six virgin priestesses continually tended and monitored her sacred fire. If any citizen wanted to leave the city and make a place for himself elsewhere, coals would be taken from the sacred hearth and used to ignite the first flame in the land where he settled.

HEBE— GODDESS OF YOUTH

The daughter of Zeus and Hera, Hebe was the goddess of youth, able to restore the spark of life in the aged and decrepit. Other than her eternal youth—of both form and spirit—she had no personality to speak of. In some myths, she was the cupbearer for the gods, keeping their cups filled with nectar during banquets.

IRIS—GODDESS OF THE RAINBOW

Iris, whose parentage is undefined, was the goddess of the rainbow. While Hermes was responsible for carrying messages from one god to another, Iris was the gods' messenger to mankind.

THE GRACES— GODDESSES OF SOCIAL INTERACTION

The three daughters of Zeus and Eurynome, daughter of the Titan Oceanus, or in some accounts the daughters of Aphrodite and Dionysus, the Graces were the deities who presided over all social functions. They always worked together.

Aglaia, the youngest of the three, was the most stately; it was Aglaia who gave a speaker the presence to captivate a crowd. Euphrosyne was the one who infused a party with good-natured laughter; without her, all parties and social functions would have been intolerably serious. Thalia, the third sister, served a double purpose, in that she was also one of the Muses; she was the spirit of comedy, the mother of the joke, however refined or crude.

ΚΑΛΛΙΟΠΗ   ΚΛΕΙΩ ΕΡΑΤΩ   ΜΕΛΠΟΜΕΝΗ

THE MUSES— GODDESSES OF ARTISTS

The daughters of Zeus and Mnemosyne, whose name means "memory," the Muses were nine in number. In early accounts they are all lumped together and not treated as separate personalities—they are thought of sim-ply as the goddesses of creative invention, hence Homer's immortal lines "Sing O Muse of the wrath of Pelleus' son Achilles" and "Tell me, Muse, of the man of many ways…" (*The Iliad* and *The Odyssey*, respectively). Later, each would be given her own personality, and special artistic endeavors would be attributed to her.

Calliope, usually depicted holding a scroll or stylus, was the Muse of epic poetry. Clio, generally portrayed holding either a scroll or

set of tablets, was the Muse of written history. Erato was the Muse of erotic poetry; Sappho, the famous female poet of Lesbos, undoubtedly owed a debt to her. Euterpe was the Muse of lyric poetry and Dionysian, rapturous music; she was most commonly pictured holding a flute, representing the musical nature of the lyric poem. Melpomene, usually depicted holding the frowning mask of tragedy and wearing the cothurnus, a high, thick-soled boot commonly worn by Greek tragic actors, was the Muse of tragedy. Polyhymnia was the Muse of religious poetry and song; her demeanor was described as pious and thoughtful. Terpsichore was the Muse of dance; like Euterpe, she was usually shown grasping a lyre. Thalia was the Muse of comedy; the opposite of Melpomene, Thalia was generally portrayed holding the classic laughing mask of comedy. Urania, typically depicted holding a globe, which served as a symbol for all the celestial bodies, was the Muse of astronomy.

Apollo and the Muses, Giulio Romano, 16th century. The Muses were Apollo's mistresses.

THE
QUEST FOR
THE GOLDEN FLEECE

THE ORIGIN OF
THE GOLDEN FLEECE

There was a king of Boeotia named Athamas who, although married to Queen Nephele—with whom he had fathered two sons, Phrixus and Leucon, and a daughter, Helle—was in love with a woman named Ino. The affair between Athamas and Ino intensified until even the servants knew of their relationship. Through hearsay, Nephele learned of the tryst. When she

The Argonauts, Costa Lorenzo,
late 15th–early 16th century.

69

Phrixus and Helle
on the back of the
golden ram. In most
accounts of this myth,
the ram is said to
have flown from
Boeotia to Colchis.
In this picture,
however, the beast
is swimming.

stricken with famine, Athamas would dispatch a messenger to the Delphic Oracle to ask for Apollo's aid and guidance.

The singed seeds didn't sprout and the fields were as barren as a desert. Desperate for guidance, Athamas sent a messenger to the Delphic Oracle. Unbeknownst to him, the messenger was in Ino's employ. On his return, the messenger told Athamas not what the Oracle had said, but the words that Ino had instructed him to say, words that would seal the doom of Prince Phrixus.

According to the messenger, the Oracle foretold that the only way to make the fields fertile again was to sacrifice the king's eldest son on top of Mount Laphystium. Even though the thought of slaying his only son sickened him, Athamas felt he had no choice. With a heavy heart, he led Phrixus to the top of the mountain. Helle followed them, pleading with her father not to kill her beloved brother.

Hera, taking notice, became enraged. For a father to kill his son because of lies from an adulterous woman was too much for her. She sent Hermes down to Boeotia with a wonderful flying ram whose fleece was made of pure gold. She told Hermes that Phrixus was to be saved and that the ram would be his ticket to safety. As the knife drew close to Phrixus' neck, Hermes appeared and placed the prince on the back of the ram. Helle, not wanting to be left behind, jumped on as well, and soon the two of them were flying away from the land that had caused them so much trouble.

Helle had great difficulty containing her excitement. She began to laugh and flail about, losing her balance over the strait that separates the landmasses that are now Asia

confronted her husband, Athamas imprisoned his queen, opening the doors of the palace and his bedchamber to Ino.

It wasn't long before Ino became obsessed with doing away with Nephele's children. She realized that if Athamas were to die, Phrixus would inherit the throne, making her position in the palace highly uncertain. She quickly devised a plan to secure her status. Ino was a princess of Thebes, a position that brought with it a great deal of respect. Knowing that the women of Boeotia held her in high regard and would do whatever she asked, Ino requested that they scorch the corn that was to be planted. Her plan was to make sure that the season's harvest never even sprouted—she knew that if the kingdom were and Europe. She fell into the water and died almost instantly. In her honor, the area was named the Hellespont.

So it was a lone boy that the golden ram brought to the kingdom of Colchis, where he was accepted by King Aeëtes as his own son. In gratitude to the gods, Phrixus sacrificed the ram to Zeus and gave the Golden Fleece to his new father, who treasured it above all things.

JASON ASSEMBLES THE ARGONAUTS

There was a time in the kingdom of Iolcus when King Cretheus died, leaving his son Aeson the throne. But Aeson's half-brother, Pelias, was ruthlessly ambitious; he usurped the throne from Aeson and imprisoned him. Unbeknownst to Pelias, however, Aeson had a son named Diomedes whom Aeson had placed in the care of the learned Centaur Chiron, a noble creature who was half-man and half-horse. Chiron took to calling the boy Jason.

When Jason was a young man, Chiron decided to tell him of his true heritage. Jason then became determined to reclaim his throne. Although now feeble with age, Pelias still possessed a sharp mind. Fearing that he might lose his ill-gained power, he consulted the oracles regularly. For years they reported nothing. But around the time Jason became aware of his lineage, Pelias was told that he should beware of a man wearing one sandal.

En route to Iolcus, Jason came to a river that proved to be an obstacle for an old woman stranded on its bank. As he was of a kind nature, Jason offered to carry the woman across. The old woman was none other than Hera in disguise; she didn't like Pelias and knew that Jason would lose one of his sandals in the mud of river if he carried a heavy load through its waters.

Now wearing only one sandal, Jason came to the city. Word soon reached Pelias that someone fitting the oracle's description had come to town. In a slight panic, Pelias ordered the man to be brought to him.

When the two met, Pelias demanded to know the traveler's identity. Jason said that in the past he was called Diomedes, and that he was the son of the king's half-brother, Aeson.

Greek krater, 5th century B.C., depicting a group of Argonauts.

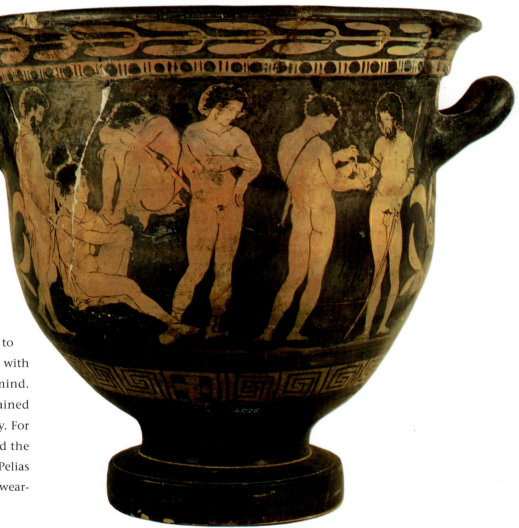

Jason then demanded that the king relinquish the throne to him, the rightful heir. Upon hearing this, Pelias knew that he had no choice, since he couldn't stand up to this athletic youth, but he was not willing to simply hand over the power.

"You will have the throne," said Pelias, "but first you must undertake a great journey. My land is haunted by the ghost of Prince Phrixus. In order to put his soul to rest, the Golden Fleece of the ram that carried him from here to the far-off land of Colchis must be found and brought back. If you bring me the Golden Fleece, I will give you the throne."

Jason accepted Pelias' proposal and soon made it known that he was looking for the bravest and noblest warriors in the land to help him in his search.

He hired the famous shipbuilder Argus to construct a vessel for the voyage; upon completion, this ship was named the *Argo*, in honor of its creator. Men from all over the world came to give Jason their aid; this assemblage of brave warriors was christened the Argonauts. Among them were such heroes as Heracles; the twins Castor and Polydeuces; the master musician and poet Orpheus; Atalanta, the huntress whose skill with a spear rivaled that of any man; and the shapeshifter Periclymenus. Echion, son of Hermes; Ascalaphus, son of Ares; Great Ancaeus, son of Poseidon; and Idmon, son of Apollo, were also members of the crew. All in all, the *Argo* had a crew of around fifty of the bravest and most gifted heroes of the ancient world.

THE QUEST

In the course of their quest, the Argonauts had many great adventures. Some of these are accorded full-length stories, others only brief mention.

THE DEATH OF HYLAS AND THE LOSS OF HERACLES

Among the first few stops of the *Argo* was a brief visit to an unnamed island to gather supplies. Shortly after the Argonauts beached, Heracles went into a nearby forest to search for a sturdy tree from which to fashion himself a new oar, since his had recently broken. After an hour or two, he came across a suitable candidate and dragged it back to camp to begin carving.

Upon his return he realized that his young squire, Hylas, was nowhere to be found. He returned to the forest to search for him, but met with failure. He found only Hylas' water pitcher, lying next to a pond. While the lad was gathering water, a group of water nymphs had surprised him. Entranced by the young man's beauty, they had dragged him down into their watery home, unintentionally drowning him. The next morning,

when Heracles still had not returned from his search, Jason decided that the *Argo* would have to sail without him.

BOXING WITH KING AMYCUS

Coming to rest on the island of Bebrycos, the Argonauts found themselves in the company of King Amycus, a belligerent man who fancied himself the greatest boxer in the world. He held such a high opinion of his skills that he challenged any and all visitors to a fight to the death.

Polydeuces, the twin brother of Castor, agreed to represent the Argonauts in the fight. A lesser man would have amended his decision when he set eyes on Amycus. The king was built like a bear, huge and muscular; the sight of him brought to mind Heracles himself. Amycus also arranged for the fight to be unfair; he supplied Polydeuces with a pair of simple leather gloves while his own were covered with sharpened steel spikes. But Polydeuces knew that an opponent of Amycus' enormous size and build would be slow and sluggish in his punches. The quick and agile Polydeuces figured the king would prove to be no great threat.

As the fight began, Polydeuces quickly recognized the weak points in Amycus' fighting style, and with one blow crushed Amycus' temple, sending bits of bone into the man's brain and killing him instantly. When Amycus' men saw their king drop to the ground dead, they raised their arms to avenge his death. The Argonauts, however, proved to be as well trained in the art of combat as Polydeuces, and the battle was soon over.

PHINEUS AND THE HARPIES

Soon the Argonauts came to eastern Thrace, where they met a seer named Phineus. Having been given the gift of prophecy by Apollo, Phineus had used his talents all too well, and had angered Zeus for predicting the future too accurately. In retribution for Phineus' "crime," Zeus had sent a band of Harpies to torment the old man.

The Harpies were evil creatures with the heads and torsos of women but the wings and talons of vultures. They had no control over their defecation and left a terrible stink wherever they went. Whenever Phineus would sit down to a meal, the Harpies would descend, snatching up what food they could and covering the rest with their droppings, making it inedible.

Phineus pleaded for help, and the Argonauts agreed to aid him any way they could. Phineus knew that the only way his curse could be lifted was with the aid of the Argonauts Calais and Zetes, the winged sons of the North Wind. The next time Phineus sat down to a meal and the Harpies darkened the skies, Calais and Zetes flew into the air after them, killing many and making the rest flee in mortal terror, never to return.

The Lemnian Women and their queen tempt Jason and the Argonauts to stay with them on the island of Lemnos. They had earlier killed their husbands and sworn to have nothing to do with men, but the beauty and valor of the Argonauts changed their minds.

The Argo approaches the Symplegades. With the aid of Phineus, the blind seer, the Argonauts were able to manuever safely past this enchanted obstacle.

THE SYMPLEGADES

That night, while sitting down to his first meal in a long time, Phineus told Jason how to maneuver the *Argo* through the Symplegades, two enormous rocks that framed the only inlet to the Bosphorus Strait. These rocks were enchanted so as to clash together unexpectedly whenever a ship passed between them, crushing the vessel and its hapless crew.

Phineus told Jason that as the *Argo* approached this magical obstacle, a dove should be released. If the bird made it through unscathed, so would the ship; if, however, the dove was not successful, Jason must give up the quest then and there, for the *Argo* would not pass through safely.

The dove made it through with the loss of only a few of its tail feathers; likewise, the *Argo* made it through with the loss of only the smallest bit of its stern. They soon landed on the shores of Colchis, land of King Aeëtes, keeper of the Golden Fleece.

COLCHIS AND THE GOLDEN FLEECE

Upon reaching the city, the Argonauts were made very welcome. Baths were drawn and a splendid feast was prepared.

After the men had eaten and were sitting around the table leisurely picking their teeth, Aeëtes asked Jason the reason for the visit. When Jason told him he was in Colchis to obtain the Golden Fleece and bring it back with him to Iolcus, Aeëtes burned inwardly; he had absolutely no intention of parting with such a prize.

By Aeëtes' silence Jason could tell that the king wasn't going to simply hand over the Fleece. Not wanting to seem ungrateful, he offered to perform any task the king might wish. Seeing the opportunity to rid his kingdom of these adventurers, Aeëtes concocted a plan: He asked Jason to plow, sow, and reap a field. The king's oxen, fire-breathing beasts famous for their malice toward men, would have to be yoked and somehow forced to plow the field. The seeds Jason was to sow were the teeth of a dragon that, when planted, would yield not corn or any other grain, but armed men ready for battle. Jason was to "harvest" this crop by emerging victorious from a battle with the Teeth-Men.

Jason agreed to Aeëtes' wishes, knowing that the next day would probably be his last. At this very moment, Medea, the king's daughter, peeked out from behind a curtain to gaze on the strangers and immediately fell in love with Jason. Overhearing what her father had planned for the beautiful young man, she vowed to help him by any means at her disposal.

Later that night, Medea sent a messenger to the *Argo*. The messenger told Jason that the king's daughter wanted to help him in his perilous endeavor, and told him where to meet Medea that night.

When the two met at the appointed place and time, Medea gave Jason a magical ointment of her own making. Once applied, this salve would make the wearer invincible for a day—the oxen would not be able to harm him. She also told him that if the Teeth-Men became too numerous, he should throw a stone in the middle of them. This would cause them to turn and fight each other until none remained.

As Medea described the ointment and the strategy of the stone, Jason found himself staring deeply into her eyes, unable to tear away. He had become as enamored of her as she was of him.

The next day there was a great gathering around the unplowed field. Jason had already applied the ointment, which flooded him with a feeling of tremendous power. When the oxen were released, he had little trouble overpowering and yoking them; their flames didn't even redden his flesh. He then guided them up and down the field, plowing the rows and sowing the teeth as he went.

When the seeds were sown, and an army of bloodthirsty men were poised for battle, Jason threw a stone in the middle of them and soon the men were fighting each other. It took only minutes for the entire army to kill one another. When the Argonauts saw the last man fall, they let out a raucous cheer. Their captain was victorious and the Fleece would soon be theirs.

Aeëtes, however, was not as pleased with the situation as were the Argonauts. He stormed back to his palace and began plotting against Jason and his men, finally deciding that he would have his army attack them that night. But Medea, knowing the way her father thought, sped to the Argo and warned Jason that he must leave soon or be ready for the worst fate her father could imagine. She told him that the Fleece was kept in a cave guarded by a horrendous dragon that never slept. She

told Jason that she would magically coax the beast to sleep, after which the Fleece could easily be taken.

While Jason went to the cave and retrieved the magnificent Fleece, Medea stole back to the palace and convinced her little brother Apsyrtus to come along with her, telling him that they were going to sail off with the Argonauts for a great adventure. The unwitting boy readily came along, and Medea and her brother were waiting on the Argo when Jason came running back to the ship, Fleece in hand.

Jason clambered back on board and gave the order to start rowing. Soon the Argo was at sea, with King Aeëtes and his best warriors in pursuit. Medea knew there was no way the Argo could outrun her father's ships; this was the reason she had brought her brother along. In an act of sheer brutality, she slew her young brother and dismembered him, flinging the pieces off the side of the ship one by one. Aeëtes, realizing what had happened, was forced to call off the pursuit in order to retrieve each piece of his young son so that he might have a proper burial.

Soon, the Argo was back at port in Iolcus. Jason gave the Golden Fleece to King Pelias and as promised, the old man stepped down, relinquishing the throne to Jason.

Jason's quest for the Golden Fleece begins with a prophecy telling his Uncle Pelias to beware a man wearing only one sandal—Jason. In most accounts, Jason loses his sandal in the muddy banks of a river while carrying a disguised Hera across. In one alternate version, however, Jason removes the sandal himself after the strap breaks en route to Iolcus.

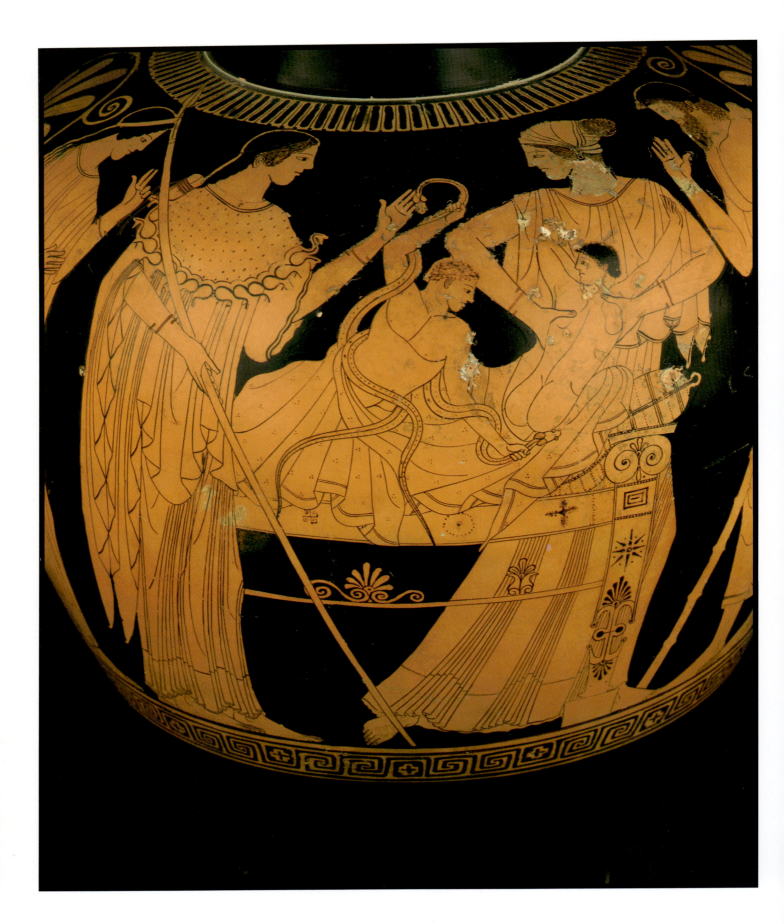

CHAPTER
XIII

THE
TWELVE LABORS
OF HERACLES

THE ORIGIN OF HERACLES

There once was a great Theban general named Amphitryon. This general's wife was Alcmene, and it was this woman whom Zeus decided would be his last mortal "diversion."

While Amphitryon was leading his army into battle with the Teleboans and Taphians, Zeus—disguising himself as Amphitryon because he knew that Alcmene was very much in love with her husband—came to

Red-figured stamnos, 4th century B.C.,
depicting the infant Heracles "playing" with
and inadvertently killing the two serpents
sent by Hera.

Alcmene's bedchamber. Before coming to Earth, Zeus had arranged for the sun not to cross the sky for three days; he had also convinced the moon to take three days to cross the sky that night. By doing this, he was sure to have enough time to lie with Alcmene as many times as he might desire.

Nine months later Zeus was strutting around Olympus, boasting that soon a son of his would be born who would rule the land of Thebes as no other king had ruled before. When Hera learned of this, she went to Zeus and made a deal with him that any prince born to the House of Perseus (the ruling family of Thebes) that night would be the next king. Zeus agreed, certain that his new son, Heracles, which means "Hera's Pride," would be brought into the world that evening.

Hera then went down to the palace of Sthenelus, whose wife, Nicippe, was seven months pregnant. Using her godly talents, Hera sped up Nicippe's labor so that the first prince born that night was not Heracles but Eurystheus, a weak, timid little soul who was as unlike Heracles as water is to fire. From the moment of his birth Heracles was destined to never be a king.

Soon after he was born, Heracles demonstrated his enormous strength. One night Hera sent two serpents into his crib to kill him. Instead of crying at the sight of the snakes, as his half-brother Iphicles did, the infant Heracles saw them as toys and began playing with them. It wasn't long before he'd accidentally killed both of the serpents. Alcmene soon discovered him looking dejectedly at the two limp things that, until a moment ago, had been so quick and playful.

During Heracles' adolescence he often had trouble containing his godlike strength. He was able to quickly master the more athletic arts, such as archery and swordplay, but when it came to academia he was rather thick. Once, during a very discouraging lyre lesson,

he grew irritated with his lack of skill and the beatings he was receiving from his teacher and, unaware of his own strength, hit the man over the head with the instrument, mistakenly crushing the teacher's skull. Amphitryon then sent him to a cattle farm where he stayed until he was eighteen, further developing his strength and skills and learning the benefits of an outdoor life.

When he was eighteen, Heracles decided to leave the farm and kill the Cithaerian Lion, because the herds he tended, as well as some neighbor's cattle, had been falling prey to this beast. He tracked the Lion to its lair on Mount Helicon and killed it in a matter of seconds. It was from this creature that Heracles got his characteristic cloak, which consisted of a lion's pelt for a cape and the head and jaws of the beast serving as an elaborate headpiece.

THE
TWELVE LABORS

During his adulthood, Heracles found himself pitted against the Minyans, who were enemies of his countrymen, the Thebans. In defense of his land, he led the attacks against the invaders and was victorious. In gratitude, King Creon of Thebes offered him the hand of his eldest daughter, Megara, which he accepted.

Hera decided that now was the time to take her vengeance. One day she sent a streak of insanity into Heracles' brain. The hero was thrown into a mad rage and slew his wife and children. When he came to his senses and realized what he had done, he secluded himself in a dark room of the palace, his mind full of the realization that the hands that cradled his crying face had also slain his family. He wanted nothing more than to kill himself. Fortunately, his longtime friend Theseus convinced him that he wasn't responsible for the

In an alternate version of the snake story, Hera sends only one serpent to kill the infant Heracles.

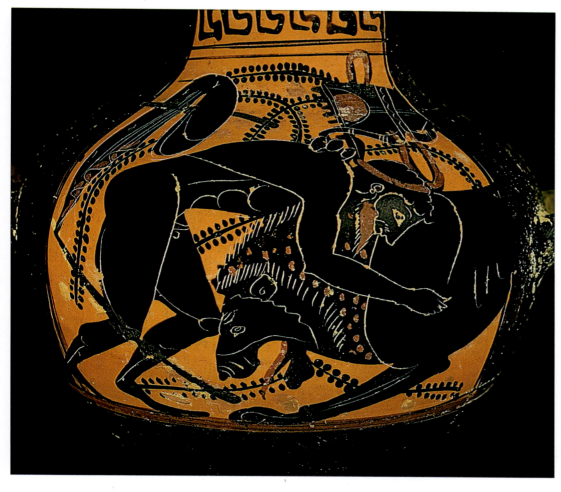

deaths because he had been insane at the time. He advised Heracles to journey to Delphi and ask the advice of Apollo's Oracle.

The Oracle told Heracles that in order to cleanse his soul, he must offer his services to King Eurystheus for twelve years. This was a repellent idea to Heracles, who considered Eurystheus to be nothing more than a weakling, undeserving of any respect. But the voice of Apollo could not be denied.

Although Eurystheus was physically weak, his mind was quite sharp, and he devised a series of twelve tasks that he felt would tax his cousin to the limits.

THE FIRST LABOR— THE NEMEAN LION

The first task was to bring back the hide of the Lion of Nemea, which was impervious to any weapon ever made.

Heracles tracked the beast to its lair on Mount Tretus. It had just returned from a kill and was sluggish with sleep and a full belly. Heracles attacked, but his weapons were of no use. The Lion, too sleepy to retaliate, sauntered into its cave and fell into a deep sleep. Heracles then blocked off the cave's exit and throttled the Lion with his bare hands. The creature awoke in a fury but soon perished under Heracles' grip. Using the Lion's own claws, Heracles flayed the beast and brought its magnificent pelt back to King Eurystheus.

THE SECOND LABOR— THE LERNAEAN HYDRA

Heracles' second task was to kill the Hydra of Lernaea, a fire-breathing, hideous-smelling reptilian monster with nine serpentine heads, one of which was immortal. Heracles' cousin Iolaus accompanied him on this journey.

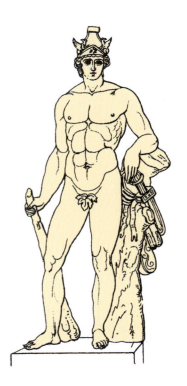

Hercules and the Hydra, Antonio Pollaiuolo, 15th century.

Seeing the trouble his cousin was in, Iolaus happened upon a brilliant idea. He quickly made a fire and soon had a makeshift branding iron glowing red hot. Firebrand in hand, Iolaus approached the battle and seared the Hydra's necks as soon as Heracles had dispatched their heads, making it impossible for new heads to sprout. Soon the Hydra was down to its last, immortal head.

Heracles cut off the immortal head with a sword and buried it, still hissing and spitting, under a gigantic boulder. Packing up to leave, Heracles noticed that the blood from the Hydra's corpse was killing everything it came into contact with. Thinking quickly, he dipped his arrows into the poisonous blood, making them the most lethal weapons in the mortal world.

Eurystheus decided that since Iolaus had helped Heracles, this task was completed unfairly. Heracles nodded his apologies, not really caring what the spindly little king thought. As far as he was concerned, the labor was finished.

THE THIRD LABOR— THE ERYMANTHIAN BOAR

Heracles' third task was to capture the invincible Boar of Erymanthia. When Heracles first saw the monster, he realized that a direct attack would result in defeat. Again, a special plan would be necessary.

Some months later, after the first snowfall, an idea came to him. After a thick blanket of white covered the land, Heracles lured the Boar into a clearing in which a huge snowbank had built up. He waited until the Boar was facing into the snowbank, then leapt out of hiding, frightening the Boar directly into the drift, where it became stuck.

Heracles bound its legs together and carried it back to Eurystheus. When the hero reached the city, the scrawny king took one look at the terrible creature on Heracles' back

Athena assisted Heracles by showing him the way to the creature's lair. She also told him that fighting the Hydra in its cave would mean his certain death; only by forcing it out into the open would he stand a chance of achieving victory.

Taking Athena's advice, Heracles sent a volley of flaming arrows into the Hydra's lair. The monster emerged screaming from the dank swamp, lunging for its tiny attacker. At first, Heracles thought he could simply bash each of the heads into oblivion, but he discovered that as soon as one was pulverized, a replacement immediately grew in its place.

and ordered his artisans to quickly fashion for him a bronze jar that would be buried in the ground, in which he could safely sit while Heracles came to town with his terrifying trophies. He also told Heracles that from now on he would have to leave all proof of his completed tasks outside the walls of Mycenae.

Passing through Iolcus en route to his fourth task, Heracles learned that Jason was amassing a small army to go off and retrieve the fabled Golden Fleece. Abandoning his labors, Heracles joined the Argonauts and returned to his labors afterward.

THE FOURTH LABOR—
THE CERYNEIAN HIND

Artemis' chariot was drawn by a team of the most beautiful hinds (female deer) ever seen, which the goddess had captured as a child. There had been one deer, however, that had eluded her; it had spied her approaching the flock and bolted, quicker than the wind, into the Ceryneian Hills. Heracles' fourth task was to capture, but not kill, this last deer. He would have to succeed where Artemis, the goddess of the hunt, had failed.

It took Heracles an entire year to locate the timid, lightning-fast animal. During that time he honed his archery skills—he'd devised a plan to take the deer alive but knew that if the plan was to meet with success, his skill with an arrow would have to rival that of Artemis herself.

After tracking the Hind to Mount Artemisium, he crouched under a bush on the grazing path that the deer walked every day. When the animal came near, Heracles shot an arrow between the tendon and bone of its front legs. The arrow passed through skin, shedding no blood. Hobbled, the deer was easy to capture. The fourth labor was finished.

THE FIFTH LABOR—
THE STYMPHALIAN BIRDS

Very few animals were sacred to Ares. It is only fitting that his sacred beasts—the Stymphalian Birds—were as foul as the Greeks found unbridled battle-lust to be. The Stymphalian Birds, so called because of their residence in the Stymphalian Swamp, were ugly creatures with beaks, talons, and wings of bronze. They had a habit of eating anyone who came near their rookery. Because there was no animal in the swamp brave enough to consider the birds as possible food, within a short time the swamp was overflowing with the foul beasts. Occasionally, groups of them would fly off in hopes of finding a new home. As they flew, they passed over countless nearby fields, befouling them with their noxious defecations, making them unfit for farming.

Clearing the Stymphalian Birds out of the marsh was Heracles' fifth labor. A single bird by itself was not terribly daunting, but Heracles was faced with countless hordes of the horrible creatures. He first went to the edge of the swamp with a great number of arrows, planning to shoot any bird that flew above the trees, thus diminishing their number to a point where the remainder could be easily dealt with.

As it turned out, the Birds were too numerous for this plan to work. Heracles could have shot a thousand in a day and it would have done no good. He prayed to Athena for guidance. Hearing his pleas, the goddess had Hephaestus create a magnificent bronze rattle that, when shaken, would fool the birds into thinking they were in the middle of an earthquake.

Positioning himself on a mountainous shelf overlooking the infested swamp, Heracles shook the rattle for all it was worth. The noise traveled down into the swamp and into the ears of the Birds, and soon the sky was black with the fleeing flocks. With nearly the entire sky full of targets, Heracles had no trouble shooting down the majority of the birds. The survivors, of which there were few indeed, worked their way east to a remote island in the Black Sea where they never caused anyone trouble again.

THE SIXTH LABOR— THE AUGEIAN STABLES

King Augeias of Elis had the largest herd of cattle the ancient world had ever known. Augeias had a bit of a tidiness problem though—no one could remember the last time the stables had been cleaned, and the manure was piled so high that it was almost impossible for a man to walk through the stables without suffocating. And the stench was so strong that it carried throughout all of the Peloponnese.

Heracles' sixth labor was to clean Augeias' stables in one day. He went to the king, told him of his task, and was met with resounding howls of laughter. Augeias, laughing so hard there were tears in his eyes, gave Heracles permission to take whatever steps necessary to get the job done. Heracles climbed to

the top of a nearby hill and noticed that two rivers, the Alpheus and the Peneius, ran nearby. He went down to the stable yard and punched two great breaches in the wall. He then went to the banks of both rivers and dug huge troughs running from their flooded banks to the stable. By diverting these rivers, Heracles cleaned out the stables in minutes.

THE SEVENTH LABOR— THE CRETAN BULL

Heracles' seventh labor was to capture the dreaded fire-breathing white bull of Crete, which had lately been rampaging through the

ABOVE: Heracles slays the Stymphalian Birds, whose beaks, talons, and feathers were made of bronze. The Birds would have torn Heracles to shreds were it not for his protective armor, the skin of the Nemean Lion.

RIGHT: Black-figured amphora, c. 4th century B.C., showing Heracles capturing the Cretan Bull.

country, burning fields, uprooting crops, and slaying the occasional passerby. When the hero arrived in Crete, King Minos offered him all the aid he might need. Heracles refused the king's kind offer, preferring to confront the animal one on one. It was a long struggle, possibly the longest single battle of his twelve labors, but Heracles was eventually successful. He muzzled the animal so that its flames were temporarily snuffed, and loaded it on a boat for the return to Eurystheus.

THE EIGHTH LABOR— THE MARES OF DIOMEDES

There once was a king of Thrace named Diomedes who had a particularly nasty habit—whenever guests would land on his shores he would offer them all the kindness and hospitality in the world, only to later feed them to his four flesh-eating horses. Heracles' eighth labor was to capture these savage animals.

Upon arriving at Diomedes' palace, Heracles was made most comfortable. Diomedes' attendants, however, soon tried to throw Heracles into the horses' pen. Heracles quickly overpowered the men, then approached Diomedes himself and, taking hold of the savage king, threw him into the pit. The eyes that had seen so many perish in that pit were now, along with the rest of him, just another meal for his treasured horses.

After that last gruesome meal, the horses' appetites became permanently sated and the beasts gave Heracles no trouble as he yoked them and brought them back to Mycenae.

THE NINTH LABOR— THE GIRDLE OF HIPPOLYTE

The Amazons were a fierce race of female warriors who held men in low regard, believing the female to be the true warrior. Their men were relegated to the common household tasks that women performed elsewhere in the ancient world. To the women went the thrill of battle and the spoils of war. It is not surprising that the Amazons had a great affinity for Ares; likewise, he had an affinity for them, so much that he gave Queen Hippolyte his sacred girdle.

Eurystheus had a daughter named Admete who desired Hippolyte's girdle. She pleaded with her father, who in turn decreed that Heracle's ninth labor would be to retrieve Hippolyte's girdle for his daughter.

Upon landing on the shores of Themiscyra, Heracles was met by Hippolyte, who found herself greatly attracted to him. Never before had she met a man who so exemplified everything she respected. He had the physical strength of a god, was steadfast in his beliefs, and was a little on the dim side. She quickly agreed to give him Ares' girdle.

Hera, observing the ease with which the charming Heracles was about to obtain the girdle, decided to complicate matters. In the guise of an Amazon, she infiltrated the city and began spreading rumors that the male stranger was planning to kidnap Hippolyte.

The Amazons were quick to come to arms. Heracles, seeing the great rush of warriors, figured he had been set up. He killed Hippolyte without a second thought, removed the girdle from her cooling corpse, and with the small army that had accompanied him, fought off the Amazons.

THE TENTH LABOR— THE OXEN OF GERYON

Geryon, the king of Tartessus, an area in what is now Spain, was reputed to be a man composed of three individual bodies, all joined at the waist. He was also known for his fabulous oxen, the finest in the world. Heracles' tenth labor was to travel to the kingdom of Geryon and return with his oxen. There was one stipulation, however: Heracles was not able to

Amazon warriors were reputed to have cut off their right breasts so that they wouldn't get in the way of their bowstrings.

barter, buy, or ask for the beasts. He had to steal them. This would, of course, invoke the wrath of the monstrous king.

Arriving in Tartessus, Heracles quickly climbed Mount Abas, where he knew the oxen were kept. There he met Orthrus, Geryon's two-headed guard dog, whom he sent to the underworld with a single stroke of his club; Eurytion, Geryon's shepherd, met with the same fate.

When word reached Geryon that his oxen were being stolen, the terrible man rose from his throne and, putting on his full armor, went out to do away with the thief. Lining himself up correctly, Heracles pierced all three of the king's bodies at once with one arrow. Geryon fell down dead and Heracles was free to take the fabulous oxen of Geryon home with him.

THE ELEVENTH LABOR— THE APPLES OF THE HESPERIDES

On Hera's wedding day, her mother, Rhea, had been so overjoyed that she presented her daughter with a tree that bore golden apples. Hera placed the tree in her garden on Mount Atlas. Since she could not be there all the time, she appointed Atlas' daughters, the Hesperides, to watch over the tree and its fruits. Some time later, Hera learned that the Hesperides were stealing the apples for their

own gain. Enraged, she dispatched the serpent Ladon to coil himself around the tree and keep a close guard over its tempting fruits.

Heracles' eleventh labor was to retrieve these apples. He decided to consult the sea god Nereus, who lived in the Po River, as to where Hera's garden was located. Nereus, it was said, would prophesy unerringly if, and only if, he was subdued physically. To make this task even more difficult, Nereus was able to change his form at will. As Heracles approached the river, he saw the sleeping Nereus snoozing soundly beneath the waves. Seeing his opportunity, the warrior jumped into the water and throttled the sea god. Nereus, now awake, immediately initiated a series of transformations, changing himself into the most horrendous creatures ever dreamed up by man or god. Heracles held on through each of these changes, and Nereus soon admitted defeat and told the hero that in order to get the apples he would have to enlist the aid of Atlas. Only Atlas, who at one time had been Hera's gardener, would be able to enter the garden. If Heracles tried to walk inside the gates, he would be killed instantly by Ladon. Nereus then pointed Heracles in the right direction and went back to his nap.

After many months, Heracles came to where Atlas, as punishment for an attempted coup against Zeus, was holding the world on his shoulders. Heracles told Atlas his problem and, much to his surprise, found Atlas willing to help, but on one condition—Heracles must take the world on his shoulders while Atlas fetched the apples.

When Atlas returned with the apples, Heracles offered the world back to him, but Atlas declined, saying that he would take the golden apples to Eurystheus for Heracles. In truth, the Titan had no intention of ever supporting the world again. Thinking quickly, Heracles asked Atlas to take the world back for only a moment so that he could relieve a kink in his neck. As soon as the Titan placed the globe back on his shoulders, Heracles made off with the apples, leaving a howling-mad Atlas in his wake.

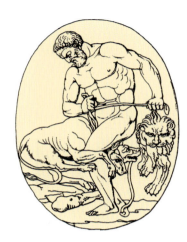

THE FINAL LABOR— THE CAPTURE OF CERBERUS

For Heracles' last labor Eurystheus decided on nothing short of the impossible. He told Heracles that he must descend into the underworld and bring to the surface the guard dog Cerberus.

Heracles asked Hermes for aid and was directed by the god of thieves to the underworld. On reaching the banks of the river Styx and being greeted with the sour face of Charon, Heracles scowled a scowl so terrible that Charon decided to forgo the usual fare he charged his patrons. He ferried Heracles to the gates guarded by Cerberus, the three-headed demon watchdog who allowed anyone into the underworld but would allow no one to leave. Realizing that it wouldn't be wise to take the beast without asking, Heracles walked past the animal to ask Hades' permission to take the creature to the surface and then return him.

Hades gave Heracles permission but stipulated that the hero could use no weapons or rope to conquer the dog, only his bare hands. Heracles returned to the gate, where he was greeted by a growling and ill-tempered Cerberus. After a lengthy battle, Heracles was able to throttle the beast long enough to take him to the surface and into the court of Eurystheus. Once the labor was officially declared completed, Heracles ran back to Hades with Cerberus on his back and promptly chained him up again. He then returned to the surface world, cleansed of the horrible crimes he had committed so many years before.

FAR LEFT: Heracles binds Cerberus, the guard dog of Hades, in order to bring him to Eurystheus for the completion of his final labor. Before taking the beast to the land of the living, Heracles requested Hades' permission to temporarily remove Cerberus from his station at the gates of the underworld.

LEFT: Statue of Hercules, Roman copy after Greek original.

THE
TROJAN WAR

THE ROAD TO WAR—
THE JUDGMENT OF PARIS

Weddings were cause for great celebration in classical times, both for mortals and for gods. Not to be invited to a wedding meant that a person wasn't considered important. When the wedding of King Peleus and Thetis, a Nereid, or water nymph, was being planned, the last person the Olympians wanted to see at the festivities was Eris, the goddess

Story of the Destruction of Troy,
studio of Colombe, c. 1500.

RIGHT: At the wedding of Peleus and Thetis, Eris, the goddess of discord, threw her infamous golden apple into the middle of the revelry, generating the famous dispute between the goddesses that led to the Judgment of Paris and eventually the Trojan War.

BELOW RIGHT: Greek amphora, 6th–5th century B.C., depicting Helen confronting Menelaus.

of discord and the sister of Ares. When Eris found out she was not going to be invited, she concocted a plan sure to throw a major upset into the goings-on.

She waited until the wedding was well under way and then threw a golden apple with the words "for the fairest" inscribed on it into the assemblage. At a mortal wedding, most people would be polite and would assume that such an offering was meant for the bride. Hera, Athena, and Aphrodite, however, all jumped for the gift at once, none of them willing to relinquish it and admit mediocrity. After much argument, they turned to Zeus to resolve the matter. Wisely, the king of the gods decided that it would be in his best interest to remain an impartial observer, for he knew that if he chose one as the fairest, the others would have no qualms about getting even with him later.

Zeus gave the job of judging to Paris, a young prince of Troy who as an infant had been exposed to die on the slopes of Mount Ida because of a prophecy that the next royal child born would be the cause of the fall of Troy. Paris had not died, however—unbeknownst to his true father, King Priam of Troy, Paris had been rescued by a shepherd who had raised the boy as his own son.

Each of the goddesses offered Paris a bribe of incredible magnitude in return for choosing her as the most beautiful. They handed

him the golden apple and told him to give the apple to the one whose proposal he liked the most. Hera offered Paris worldly rule over all of Europe and Asia; if he had taken her offer, it would have resulted in the largest empire ever conceived. Athena promised the young lad victory over the Greek army, total conquest of the Trojans' enemies. But Aphrodite, realizing that Paris was a young boy with the majority of his thoughts not on world domination but on softer, more personal victories, offered him the most beautiful woman in all the world: Helen, the wife of Menelaus, king of Sparta.

Even though Paris was involved with a beautiful nymph at the time, he had heard stories of Helen's beauty and found himself intoxicated at the idea of having her. He quickly handed over the golden apple to

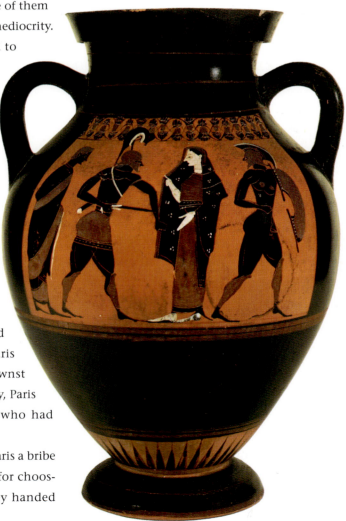

Aphrodite, who now, even though the judgment was not based solely on merit, could call herself the fairest of the Olympians.

Following the Judgment, Paris returned to Troy to compete in the annual games held in honor of Priam's "dead" son (who was, in fact, Paris himself). During the course of these games, Paris' true identity was revealed to his father and brothers, and the young prince was accepted back into the fold. Soon after this, Paris went to Sparta, home of Menelaus and Helen, where his bribe was paid: Helen fell in love with him, and the two returned to Troy. (It is sometimes said that she was abducted, but there is much evidence to the contrary.)

Paris and Helen's relationship led to the Trojan War, the longest, most brutal, and most romanticized war in the classical canon. And at the true moment of birth of this war, we find a vain and stubborn goddess.

The Love of Paris and Helen, Jacques Louis David, 1788.

THE
TROJAN WAR

After Paris was transported by Aphrodite to Sparta, he was made most welcome by King Menelaus and Queen Helen. Menelaus soon announced that he must leave to tend to

White-figured
skyphos, c. 490 B.C.,
showing Greek heroes
discussing the siege
of Troy.

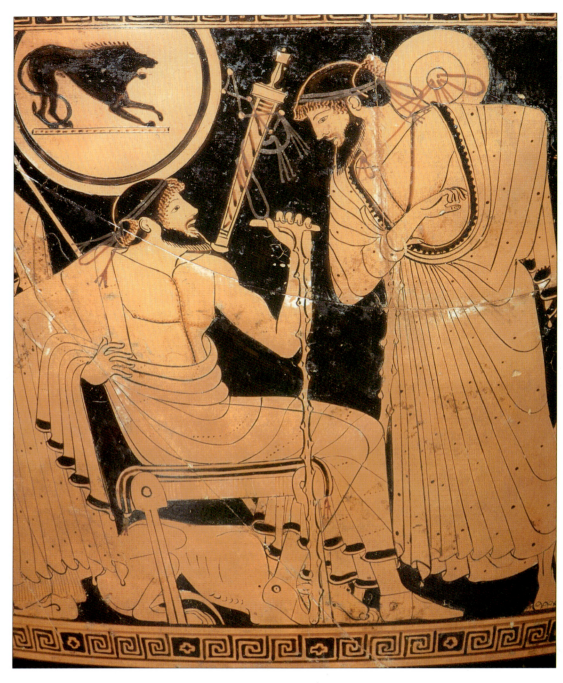

some unfinished business on Crete. During his absence he entrusted his home to his new Trojan friend. The night after Menelaus left, Paris seduced Helen on the island of Krani, en route back to Troy, where Paris promised her she would soon be his wife.

Upon his return, Menelaus sent out a call to all the kings and allies of Greece. He knew they would reply because they had all courted Helen and sworn an oath, forced upon them by Tyndareus, Helen's stepfather (her true fa-

ther was Zeus). Tyndareus had been worried that as soon as one man had won Helen's hand, her slighted suitors would retaliate violently. To put his fears to rest, he had made each suitor swear to defend the house of Helen's eventual husband, whoever he might be, if wrong was ever done to him because of the marriage. When word of Menelaus' situation reached the royalty of Greece, they called their armies together to travel to Troy and reclaim Helen.

The fleet assembled at Aulis, on the northern coast of Greece. Agamemnon, king of Mycenae, was chosen as leader. Under him was a cast of heroes: his brother Menelaus; Odysseus, king of Ithaca; Achilles, king of the Myrmidons; Achilles' friend and companion, Patroclus; Greater Ajax; Lesser Ajax; Diomedes, king of Argos; Teucer the archer, half-brother of Greater Ajax; and Nestor, who was considered the wisest of the assembled men. In all, there were 100,000 men in the Greek army; the fleet consisted of 1,186 ships. It was an army the like of which had never been seen.

When all was ready, the men sat down for a final feast before setting sail. During the meal a snake climbed a nearby tree and devoured eight baby sparrows and the mother bird. The snake then turned to stone. Calchis, the army's prophet, interpreted this to mean that the war against Troy would rage for ten years, the total number of living things that died on the tree. The first nine years would be futile, with nothing gained for either side, but the tenth year would end with the fall of Troy.

The fleet soon reached Troy, which was located on the northeastern coast of what is now Turkey. And as Calchis had foretold, nothing significant happened for nine years. The sheer vastness of the Greek army mattered little against the indomitable walls of Troy. Inside the city, King Priam, Queen Hecuba, Paris, and Helen all wondered how long the siege would last.

Hector, son of Priam and brother of Paris, was the mightiest of the Trojan warriors. Only

Achilles was a fair match for him. The most tragic event of the Trojan War centered around these two warriors. It was this story of the frailty and stubbornness of human pride that Homer told in *The Iliad*, an epic tale that depicts fifty-one days of the Trojan War and the consequences of one man's selfish dignity.

Homer's epic begins at the start of the war's tenth year. Both sides are weary of fighting. The whole war seems to be an exercise in futility. The touchstone for the tragedy is, as the first line of the poem says, "the wrath of Peleus' son Achilles." During a meeting of the Greek leaders, Agamemnon is approached by an old man named Chryses, a priest of Apollo. During a raiding party on the nearby island of Tenedos, Chryseis, the old man's daughter, had been taken away to become Agamemnon's concubine. Out of love for his child, Chryses had come to plead with the king, but Agamemnon sent him away without a second thought. Chryses, calling on Apollo, demanded that justice be served. Apollo, who was quite willing to help so loyal a priest, sent a deadly plague upon the Greek forces.

Agamemnon asked Calchis for aid. The seer said that the plague would be lifted when the daughter of Apollo's priest was returned to her father. Agamemnon immediately sent Chryseis back to Tenedos, and the plague soon ended.

A meeting was then called in which Agamemnon informed his colleagues that since his bedmate had been taken from him, he required another. As a replacement, he chose Briseis, Achilles' concubine. Enraged

FAR LEFT: Calchis the seer predicts that the war with Troy will last ten years.

ABOVE: Paris' character has been a matter of dispute for years. Was he a classic hero who sacrificed all for love, or was he a cowardly seducer who stole an unwilling Helen to satisfy his lust?

LEFT: Paris introduces Helen to his father, King Priam of Troy, while Cassandra, Paris' sister, predicts that Helen will bring ruin to their city.

that Agamemnon could care so little about the happiness of his generals, Achilles decided, from that point on, to abstain from the war. He had been slighted by his leader and therefore felt that he no longer owed him allegiance. He retreated to his tent, where he was consoled by his longtime friend and companion, Patroclus.

That night Thetis, Achilles' mother, visited her angry son. She learned of the wrong her son had suffered and became infuriated. She flew to Olympus to demand Zeus' aid. She implored the king of the Gods to give quick and decisive victory to the Trojans.

At this time all of Olympus was buzzing about the war. It had become such an item of conversation that the gods had chosen sides. Zeus favored the Trojans, but kept it a secret from Hera, who favored the Greeks. Athena wanted to see the downfall of the Trojans. Aphrodite sided with the Trojans, and Ares, who was for the most part incapable of original thought, wanted whatever Aphrodite wanted. Poseidon sided with the Greeks. Apollo and Artemis favored the Trojans. Zeus answered Thetis' request. He sent a dream to Agamemnon, promising him victory if he attacked the next day. Zeus knew that without Achilles, the Greeks had no hope of winning.

The next day, in the middle of the battle, the armies ceased fighting and spread apart. A decision had been reached to let the two warriors whose hearts were closest to the actual cause of the war fight it out between them. Menelaus and Paris soon advanced on each other. Paris threw a spear that was easily deflected by Menelaus. The king of Sparta then threw his own spear, which nicked the prince of Troy. Menelaus charged, grabbed hold of Paris' helmet, and flung the man around by the head. A dizzy Paris soon found himself being dragged toward the Greek camp. Victory was within reach, but Aphrodite caused Paris' helmet strap to break, freeing him. She then swept him up in a cloud and returned him inside the walls of Troy.

Seeing what had happened, Agamemnon declared the battle over. The Greeks had won. He promised no more blood would be spilled if the Trojans surrendered and returned Helen to Menelaus. It seemed certain that the Trojans were going to surrender.

Hera, who was determined that the war shouldn't end until the walls of Troy lay in ruin, dispatched Athena to start things up again. Athena flew to the battlefield and convinced a young Trojan named Pandalaus to take aim at Menelaus with his bow. He wounded the king, incurring the wrath of the Greeks, who now would be satisfied only with the total obliteration of Troy.

The next significant battle was between Diomedes and Hector. The two were going at it tooth and nail when Diomedes realized that Ares was fighting alongside Hector, guiding his blows. His first reaction was unabashed fear, but Hera soon came to him and convinced him that he was a better fighter than Ares. Taking strength from her words and from Athena's guiding hand, Diomedes launched a spear that pierced the god of war. Ares let out a bellow of such fury that, for a moment, all fighting on the battlefield stopped.

Ares flew up to Zeus and complained about the treatment he had just received. Zeus had no pity for the cowardly god and ordered him to remove himself from the fighting. With Ares gone, the Trojans felt much less enthusiastic about the battle and retreated back inside the protective walls of their city. Zeus then remembered his promise to Thetis and went to Earth to hasten the Trojan victory.

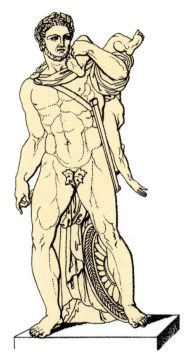

OPPOSITE: *Jupiter and Thetis*, Ingres, 1811.

ABOVE: Hector returns from battle carrying the dead body of a Greek warrior over his shoulder.

LEFT: King Menelaus and Paris engage in battle. Menelaus would have dragged Paris into the Greek camp if Aphrodite had not transported the young prince back inside the walls of Troy.

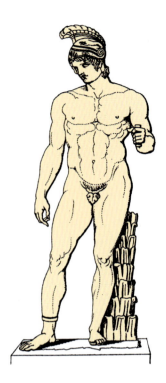

ABOVE: The warrior Achilles, whose wrath and stubbornness caused the death of many Greek soldiers.

RIGHT: Greater Ajax wounds Hector before the walls of Troy. Apollo healed Hector's wound quickly so that the Trojans would not become disheartened.

The next battle was a near-disaster for the Greeks. With Achilles still refusing to fight, and with Zeus supporting the enemy, the Greeks soon found themselves pushed back to their ships. Luckily for the Greeks, night fell and the battle ended. Their position, however, was less than desirable.

While the wine flowed in abundance in Troy that night, in the Greek camp remorse was the intoxicant. Agamemnon was near the point of giving up and sailing home. Nestor persuaded him that if he would simply apologize to Achilles and return Briseis to him, things would change. With Achilles fighting once again for the Greeks, the Trojans would not be able to duplicate the ferocious attack they had managed that day. After some reflection, Agamemnon realized he had been foolish. He asked Odysseus to go to the noble warrior and relay his apology.

Achilles received Odysseus graciously. Food was served and the conversation was friendly and most enjoyable. But when Odysseus told Achilles of Agamemnon's apology, the conversation turned cold. Achilles told Odysseus that Agamemnon could offer a thousand apologies and it still wouldn't be enough. He continued to refuse to fight.

The next day the fighting picked up exactly where it had left off. Soon it became evident that the Trojans were going to win. When Hera realized this, she devised a plan. She came across her husband on top of Mount Ida, watching the carnage below. With her soothing words and caresses, Hera seduced Zeus into lying with her. For a while Zeus forgot about the battle, giving the weary Greeks the advantage they needed.

Soon the tide of the battle turned. Greater Ajax had wounded Hector, greatly disheartening the Trojans. The Greeks were fighting with renewed fury, urged on by a supportive Poseidon.

When he awoke on Mount Ida, Zeus realized what had been done and became enraged. Seeing the wounded Hector lying gasping on the field, he ordered Apollo to amend the situation quickly. The god of healing quickly revived the fallen Trojan. With Apollo by his side, a renewed Hector once again leapt into the fray, turning the tide once again for the Trojans. They fought furiously, pushing the Greeks farther and farther back until it became evident that the Greek ships would be set aflame.

Meanwhile, in Achilles' tent, Patroclus could no longer remain idle. He convinced Achilles to trade armor with him. By dressing as the Greeks' greatest warrior, Patroclus was sure he culd fool the Trojans into believing that Achilles had reentered the battle, which would greatly discourage them, possibly even turning the advantage back to the Greeks. Achilles, still refusing to fight, agreed to Patroclus' urgings. The ruse was immediately successful; Patroclus entered the fray, and soon the tide was turned. The Trojans shrank in fear from the sight of an enraged Achilles, and soon no warrior would even approach the disguised Patroclus except Hector.

Even though Patroclus fought valiantly and with a skill he had not known he had, he was still no match for Hector. The prince of Troy quickly dispatched Patroclus to the underworld by letting loose with a well-aimed spear. In mockery of his fallen enemy, Hector stripped Patroclus of Achilles' armor, which he then donned himself.

It was Antilochus, the son of Nestor, who brought the bad news to Achilles. While the death of hundreds of his countrymen had not been enough to bring Achilles out of his tent, the death of his friend was. Embittered and enraged, he vowed to avenge the death of Patroclus. Thetis, hearing this, asked Hephaestus to fashion for Achilles a new set

of armor. This armor was so glorious that when Achilles took to the field the next day, the Trojans were filled with dread.

Never before had Achilles raged so furiously. He cut down men before they even knew he was upon them. Even the waters of the fierce river Scamander were not able to stop Achilles' advance. He was filled with an impossible fury. He wouldn't rest until Patroclus was avenged. The Trojans were soon filling the walls of their city, for their advances had turned into retreats under the mighty arm of Achilles. Soon there was only one Trojan not within the safety of the walls—Hector stood in Achilles' old armor beneath the walls of Troy, spear and sword at the ready.

Athena, who was fighting alongside Achilles, made herself visible to Hector. Seeing that Athena herself was against him, Hector's strong resolve faded. Achilles chased Hector around the walls of Troy three times. Eventually, Athena, growing bored of such childishness, appeared before Hector in the form of his brother Deiphobus. Thinking he now had an ally, Hector stopped running and turned to face Achilles. He tried to strike a deal with Achilles, suggesting that the victor should return the loser's body to the appropriate camp.

Achilles spat at Hector's offer, his rage and grief over the loss of Patroclus not forgotten. Spears were thrown by both men, but only Achilles' aim was true. He stripped Hector's cooling corpse of its armor, pierced Hector's feet, threaded them with a rope that he tied to the back of his chariot, and dragged the

ABOVE: Achilles drags Hector's body around the walls of Troy while Hermes gathers Hector's soul for its trip to Hades.

RIGHT: White-figured skyphos, 5th century B.C., depicting Priam begging Achilles for Hector's body.

body around the walls of Troy, an added indignity. After Achilles' wrath had died and Hector's body lay in the Greek camp, Priam went to the Greek hero and pleaded for the return of his son's body.

Achilles was deeply moved by the old man's words. In Priam's grieving he recognized the universality of death, realizing that all men would lose those close to them, that his loss of Patroclus was no more painful

For nine days Troy grieved over Hector, and for those same nine days the Greeks grieved the loss of Patroclus. Both were buried. It was a wiser and kinder Achilles that knew both his days and those of Troy were now short in number. At this point *The Iliad* comes to a close. The Trojan War, however, does not.

Achilles was soon killed by none other than Paris. After Achilles' birth, Thetis had taken her infant son to the river Styx and dipped the newborn in its waters, thereby

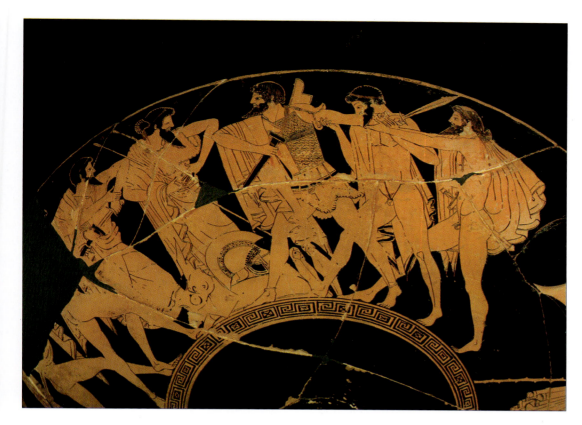

making him invulnerable except for his ankle, which was the spot where she had held him when she dipped him in the river. It was at this vulnerable spot where Paris' arrow, guided by the hand of Apollo, had pierced the hero's flesh; Achilles died from an infection soon after.

The glorious arms of Achilles, fashioned by Hephaestus himself, were now a matter of contention among the Greeks. Who should rightly receive the armor? Much discussion was held, and the choice was narrowed down to either Odysseus or Greater Ajax. After a vote, the arms went to Odysseus.

Feeling that he had been disgraced, Ajax became determined that both Agamemnon and Menelaus should die. That night, as he approached their tents, he went slightly mad. He wandered until he came to the area where the Greeks kept their flocks of sheep. In his deranged state, he thought the sheep to be a collection of Greek soldiers. He ran pell-mell into the flock and began slaughtering them at random. He then singled out the sheep he

thought to be Odysseus and brought it back to his tent, where he beat the poor creature with his fists until only a bloody bag of broken and crushed bones remained. His senses were then returned to him. Realizing what he had just done, he threw himself upon his sword, unable to face the disgrace he had brought upon himself.

The Greeks were now very distraught. Two of their finest warriors had perished in a short time. They wondered if victory would ever be attained.

The Greeks then learned through a prophet that Troy would survive until a fabulous statue of Athena was taken from within its walls. Odysseus and Diomedes decided that they must steal the statue. In the dark of night, Odysseus helped Diomedes scale the walls. Diomedes quickly located the statue and brought it back to the Greek camp.

Their spirits now lifted, the Greeks decided the time had come for action. It was Odysseus who realized that the only way to be certain of a victory would be to get the

Greek army inside the walls of Troy. He set his mind to the problem and soon came up with the most celebrated example of strategic thinking in the history of war.

Odysseus ordered that a gigantic, hollow wooden horse be built. His plan was for soldiers to hide inside the belly of the horse, which would be left outside the gates of Troy. The Greek ships would sail off, giving the Trojans the impression that they had given up, and that the horse was a gift symbolizing their surrender.

The morning of Troy's last day was one of both confusion and rejoicing. The sight of the gigantic horse outside the city caused some citizens to recoil in terror. But when it was discovered that the Greek camp was empty and the ships were gone, the fright turned into celebration. When some Trojan soldiers examined the remains of the Greek camp, they found a lone soldier remaining. His name was Sinon, and he had been thoroughly coached by Odysseus as to what to tell the Trojans when he was discovered.

He told them that he had been chosen as a sacrifice for Athena, who was angry that her statue had been stolen. He was certain he was going to die, he told the Trojans, but had escaped at the last minute and found refuge in a nearby marsh. When questioned about the horse, he told them that it too was meant as an offering to Athena, a replacement for the statue Diomedes had stolen. The reason it was so large, he said, was so that they would be loath to bring it into the city, thereby incurring the wrath of Athena.

The gullible Trojans believed every word of Sinon's story, just as Odysseus knew they would. In order to appease Athena, they brought the horse inside the walls of Troy and, as night was falling, decided to wait until morning to figure out what they should do with it. That night, while all the citizens of Troy slept soundly for the first time in ten years, a trapdoor opened in the horse and the hidden Greek soldiers emerged. They set fire to many of Troy's buildings, and when the sleepy Trojan soldiers ran to the streets wondering what was going on, they were cut down one by one.

The next morning, the only movement in the once proud city of Troy came from the wisps of smoke curling skyward from the dying coals. The men had all been killed. The women had been corralled on the beach to be divided among the Greeks and taken home as slaves. The children were either slain or left to die. The Greeks, victorious after ten long years, boarded their ships and set sail for home. The Trojan War was over.

Seven of the principal heroes of the Trojan War (from left): Menelaus, Helen's husband; Paris, Helen's lover; Diomedes, the leader of the Greeks during Achilles' absense; Odysseus, whose exploits are detailed in *The Odyssey*; Nestor, the wise elder king of Pylos; Achilles, the mightiest of the Greeks; and Agamemnon, the leader of the Greek army.

The Trojans bring the horse inside the city. In the foreground, the Trojan priest Laocoön and one of his sons are killed by a serpent sent by Apollo. Laocoön had tried to warn the Trojans of the true nature of the horse but was silenced by the serpent's coils.

THE
TRAVELS OF ODYSSEUS

The story of the warrior Odysseus' attempts to get back home to Ithaca after the Trojan War is told solely by Homer, in *The Odyssey*. This epic poem begins after the fall of Troy. During the war, Athena had aided the Greeks, but when her temple was ransacked by Diomedes and Odysseus, she became determined that no Greek would return home from Troy, and asked Poseidon for aid in her vengeful plot. The sea god whipped up such a storm that the recently departed Greek ships were thrown and tossed about on the

The Odyssey, Ingres, 1827. This painting is not a depiction of any particular person but a personification of Odysseus' epic journey.

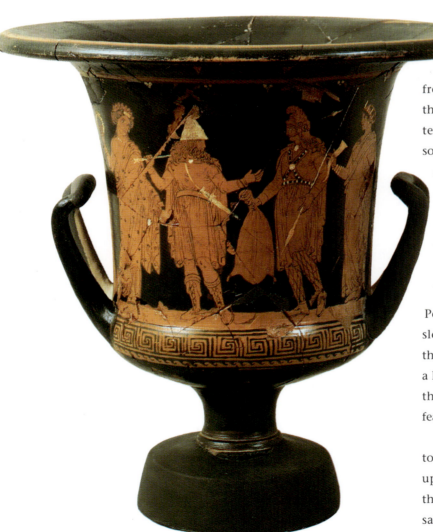

Italian krater, 5th–4th century B.C., depicting Ulysses (the Roman version of Odysseus) giving wine to Polyphemus.

violent sea. Many ships and many men were lost. A few survived, however, and did return home, despite Athena's wishes.

Such was not the case for Odysseus, the king of Ithaca. His ships were tossed by the storm to the island of Ismarus, where he led a raid on the inhabitants, the Cicones. Odysseus underestimated the strength of his opponents and suffered a sizable loss of seventy-two men. Leaving Ismarus, Odysseus set course to sail around the southeastern tip of the Pelopennese. This was the most direct route back to Ithaca. But again Poseidon threw the ships off-course, this time blowing them around for nine days until they came to the northern coast of Africa. Here Odysseus

discovered a race of men who ate the fragrant blossoms of the lotus plant, which caused them to fall into an opiated state. Some of Odysseus' men fell under the flower's spell and had to be forcibly removed lest they forever forget their homeland, still so far away.

They soon beached beneath the mouth of an enormous cave. Around the cave was a fence that served as a containing wall for a sizable number of sheep, all very fat and obviously well tended. Realizing that whoever tended the sheep might possibly give food, rest, and aid to the weary sailors, Odysseus set off with twelve of his men and a full wine-skin—an offering of friendship to the unknown shepherd.

The cave contained a wealth of food. Milk pails were everywhere, filled to the brim. Meat, dried and fresh, hung from the walls. Everywhere was something that made the mouths of the tired sailors water. And since no one was home, they were soon feasting to their heart's content. Bloated and slothful from the meal, they hardly noticed the huge shape that soon blocked the entranceway. It was the Cyclops Polyphemus, a son of Poseidon, and he was in no way pleased to see his home pillaged by humans.

Before Odysseus could do anything, Polyphemus had snatched up a few of the slowest sailors and bashed in their skulls on the floor of the cave. The monster then rolled a large rock in front of the entrance, blocking the only escape route. He then took his time feasting on the still-warm bodies.

When Polyphemus left the next morning to tend his flock, Odysseus had time to come up with a plan. When the Cyclops returned that evening he once again slew and ate some sailors. Odysseus approached the monster while he was heavy with food and offered him a cup of the wine he had brought. Poly-

phemus, who had never before tasted wine, downed it instantly and demanded another cup, then another and another. Soon, the monster had passed out drunk.

Odysseus' men took up the large pointed stick they had fashioned earlier and rammed it deep into Polyphemus' only eye. The monster woke up howling and frantically groped around the floor of the cave, searching for his attackers. He met with no luck, though, since Odysseus had ordered his men to hide under Polyphemus' sheep. The Cyclops rolled the enormous rock aside, figuring the humans would be easy to find as they ran out through the opening.

All he felt, however, were the backs of his sheep; he never thought to search underneath them. As soon as the men were out of Polyphemus' reach, they emerged from their hiding places, ran back to the ships, and set sail, leaving a raging Polyphemus behind.

Poseidon's hatred of Odysseus grew a thousandfold. He now had a personal vendetta against Odysseus and no longer needed to be asked by Athena to cause him trouble. But by this time Athena had forgotten her anger toward the Ithacan king. Quite the opposite—she had remembered her fondness for his cunning and intelligence and found herself liking him more with each passing day.

The next area Odysseus came to was the floating island of Aeolia, home of Aeolus, the keeper of the winds. Aeolus received the travelers with open arms and a full table, and

Black-figured vasepainting, 6th century B.C., showing Odysseus and three companions blinding Polyphemus.

TOP RIGHT: *Neptune and Ulysses' Ship*, Tibaldi Pellegrino, 16th century.

BOTTOM RIGHT: Circe the witch changes Odysseus' crewmen into pigs. She later relented out of love for Odysseus and changed them back.

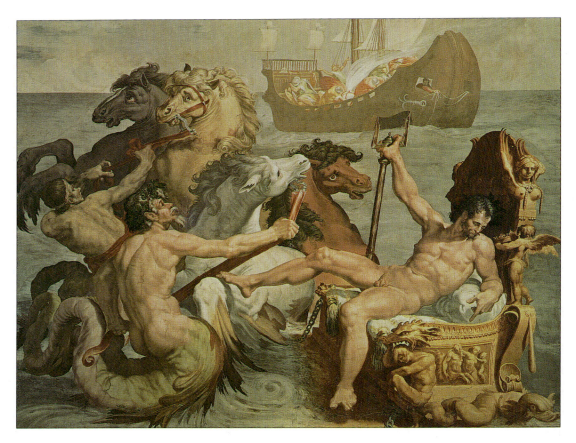

proved to be a most accommodating host. On Odysseus' departure, Aeolus gave the king a leather bag that contained all the western winds that might blow Odysseus' ships off-course once again. Odysseus was overjoyed; without the western winds to hinder their journey, his ships would reach Ithaca in a mere nine days.

Once under way, some of Odysseus' crew figured that the bag must contain a great treasure. They stole the bag from under Odysseus' protective gaze and opened it, freeing the western winds. Immediately, the ships were once again blown off-course.

After many days, Odysseus' remaining twelve ships came to the land of Lamus, home of the Laestrygones, a race of cannibalistic giants who, upon seeing the twelve ships enter their harbor, smashed eleven of them. Luckily, Odysseus was on the twelfth ship, which had not yet entered the harbor.

With the majority of his fleet destroyed, Odysseus' heart was heavy; so it was without

hesitation that he beached on the island of Aeaea, home of the seductive witch Circe. Odysseus sent a scouting party to see what dangers lay on the island.

When they encountered Circe, the members of the scouting party were so entranced by her beauty that they had no idea that the drinks she was offering them were in reality potions of her own devious making. No sooner had the men downed the drinks than they were turned into pigs. As an added indignity, Circe made sure that the potions didn't erase the men's memories. They had the bodies of pigs but retained the minds of men.

One member of the party, however, was lucky enough to escape; he returned to Odysseus with word of what had happened. Fearing for his men, Odysseus went off alone to meet the witch. En route he encountered a youth, actually Hermes in disguise, who gave him an herb that he said would protect him from Circe's magic.

When Odysseus, who had already eaten the herb and knew himself to be protected, met Circe, he took the cup she offered and quaffed it. When he remained unchanged, Circe's eyes widened and her mouth fell open. Never before had she met anyone who was immune to her magic. Odysseus then threatened to run her through with his sword if she did not return his men to their natural forms at once. She immediately complied, but not because of Odysseus' sword—she had fallen in love with the wanderer.

As soon as all the men were changed back to their proper forms, Circe became the most accommodating of hostesses. Odysseus realized that she wasn't as evil as he first had thought, and since the men were very tired and needed a rest, he decided they should stay with Circe for a while. After a year had passed, he felt it was time once again to set sail and so, with a heavy heart, he bid farewell to the sorceress.

Before they left, Circe told him what he must do if he wished to return home safely. What she told him was no easy or pleasant task—he must travel to the underworld and find the spirit of the blind prophet Tiresias, the only person who could tell Odysseus and his men how best to reach their beloved homeland. She also told Odysseus how to lure Tiresias' spirit out from its eternal rest. When he came to the underworld, he heeded Circe's advice and dug a deep pit. He then slaughtered many sheep and bled them into the fresh chasm; soon the hole was filled to the rim with steaming, fresh blood. The scent of the blood lured many spirits out from their rest, and soon Odysseus found himself surrounded by countless moaning ghosts, all longing to quench their thirst. He saw many of his fallen comrades that horrible day, including the ghost of brave Achilles and that of mighty Ajax, who was still angry about losing Achilles' armor to Odysseus. He saw the spirit of

LEFT: Odysseus speaks with the spirit of Tiresias in the depths of Hades.

BELOW: Attic vase, 5th century B.C., showing Odysseus (left) pursuing Circe (right).

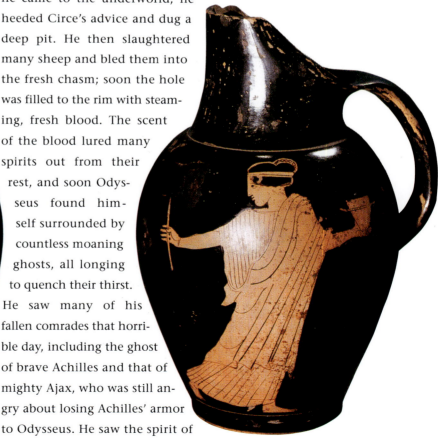

his mother, Antikleia, and his friend Agamemnon. But heeding the words of Circe, he held them all off until he spied the visage of Tiresias. He then directed the spirit to the pit and let it drink its fill of the pungent froth. After Tiresias' thirst was quenched, Odysseus asked him how he might return to Ithaca.

The ghost told him that all would be well as long as none of his crewmen harmed the oxen of Helios, the god of the sun, at whose island they would soon arrive. He then told Odysseus to take heart, for even though many troubles might lie before him, he would eventually reach his beloved home and family. Odysseus returned to the surface world, letting the countless ghosts gorge themselves on the pool of blood.

Odysseus again set sail, stopping on the way at Circe's island to tell her what had happened. She informed him that soon he would come upon the island of the Sirens. The Sirens were fearful creatures, she told him, but not in the usual ways. They were quite beautiful and had voices radiant with life when they sang. It was their singing that Odysseus should beware. Once again, Circe told Odysseus how to overcome the next obstacle he was certain to encounter.

Taking her advice, Odysseus lashed himself to the mast of his ship as soon as it neared the fateful island. In order to prevent the rest of the crew from falling under the spell of the Sirens' song, he made each man plug his ears with cotton. The nearer they came to the Sirens' island the more Odysseus realized why these women should be feared. He saw, scattered all around their tiny islet, the wreckage of countless ships and the skeletons of their crews. The men, so intoxicated by the beauty of the Sirens' singing, had run their ships full force into the jagged reef that surrounded the island, smashing their boats to pieces. Odysseus himself was not immune to their song, and he found himself struggling to get free of the binding ropes. As the songs faded away into the distance, he found his senses returning, and was amazed at the power of the wondrous music.

The ship's next peril was the dual danger of Scylla and Charybdis, two terrible sister monsters. According to legend, whoever passed safely by one would undoubtedly fall prey to the other. Scylla had twelve legs and six heads, with each mouth containing three sets of terrible teeth. Charybdis, whose body is never described, lived beneath the water and three times a day sucked a great amount of water into her mouth, only to spit it back out again. By doing this she created whirlpools so fierce that even Poseidon couldn't stop their formation. With the aid of the now helpful Athena, Odysseus was able to maneuver past both monsters, but only after losing six of his crewmen.

The tired men next came to Island of the Sun, home of Helios. When the men saw Helios' magnificent oxen they forgot Tiresias' warning and, tired of eating only fish, killed some of the sacred oxen and feasted on the flesh. Odysseus ate none of the meat, knowing full well that to do so spelled death. When the ship left the island, Helios was quick to avenge the trespass. With a bolt of thunder he tore the ship apart, killing the sailors. Odysseus was the sole survivor, and was carried by the waves to an island ruled by the Nymph Calypso. Here he stayed for many years, unable to leave because Calypso had no ships at her disposal.

On Olympus, Athena pleaded with Zeus to give Odysseus aid since he had proven himself a worthy mortal on his many adventures. Zeus agreed and sent Hermes to Calypso with the message that she was to help Odysseus in any way possible. With a heavy heart, Calypso, who had fallen in love with Odysseus, gave him the timber needed to construct a raft and provided him with provisions for his

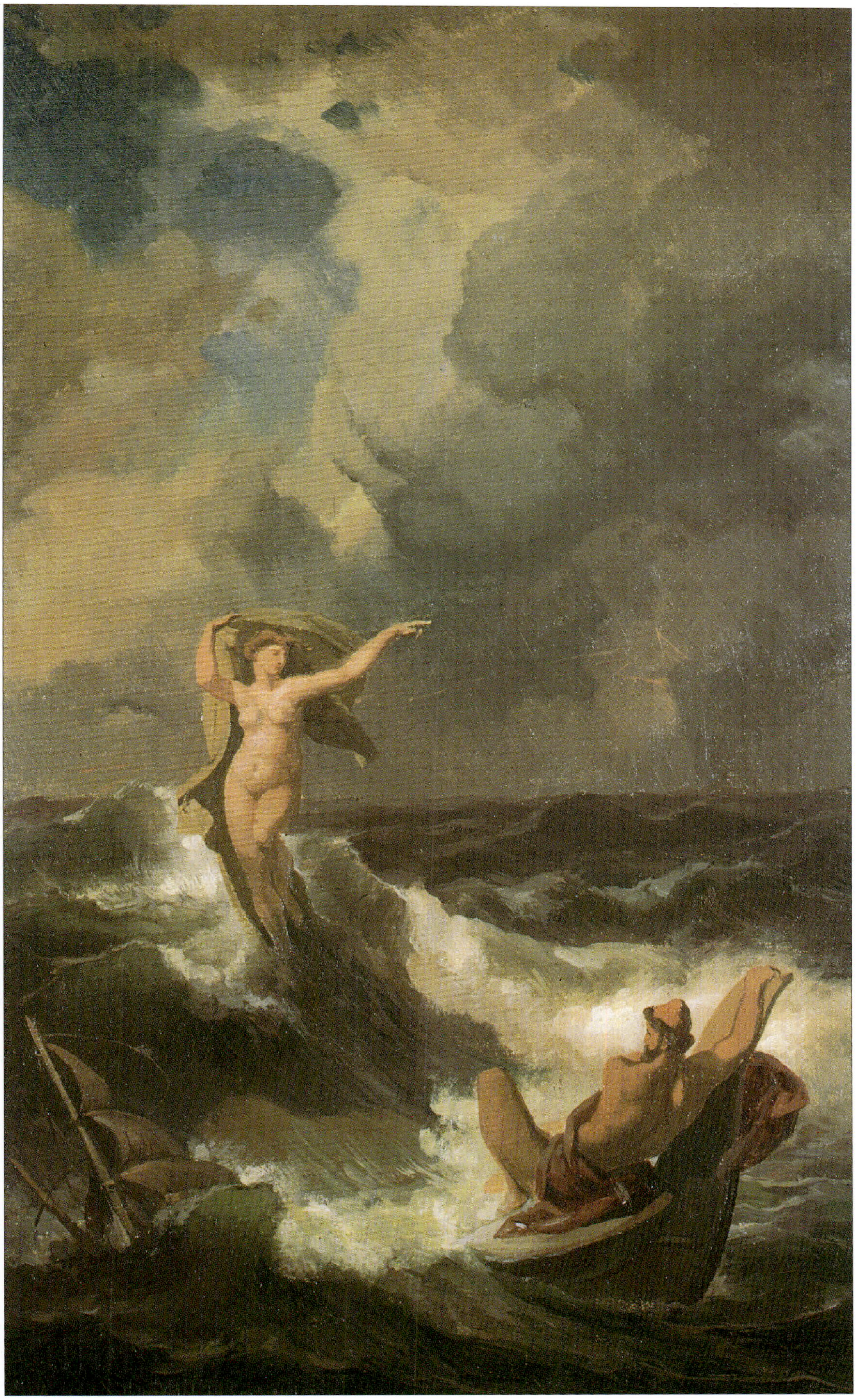

Ulysses and the Siren, Friedrich Preller, 1832–1834.

journey home. His heart filled with joy, he set sail on his flimsy raft for Ithaca, nine years after the fall of Troy.

Seeing Odysseus on the ocean's surface, Poseidon immediately whipped up another fierce storm. The raft was destroyed, throwing Odysseus into the turbulent sea. He would have died if the sea goddess Leucothea hadn't come to his aid, telling him to swim until he reached land. She also gave him her veil, which would protect him from both drowning and sharks.

Two days later Odysseus awoke to find himself on the shores of Phaeacia. He was discovered by Nausicaa, the daughter of King Alcinous, who told him to go to the palace and ask Queen Arete for help, since her father never refused anything her mother asked. Odysseus did as he was told and soon found himself well taken care of. To repay the royal family's kindness and generosity, he told them of his many adventures.

Because Odysseus' journeys had kept him away from Ithaca for nineteen years, most people thought him dead. Only Penelope and Telemachus, Odysseus' son, believed he was alive. Unfortunately, many young men had come to vie for Penelope's hand. Convinced the king would never return, these men had no qualms about raiding the royal larder and using the palace to their own ends.

To keep the many suitors at bay, Penelope told them she was busy weaving a burial shroud for her father, who had recently died, and could not see anyone. Since this was a noble cause, none of the suitors challenged its validity. But it was, of course, a ruse. Every night, Penelope unraveled what she had woven that day, so that she never made any progress. This trick worked for a while, but eventually one of the suitors caught her in the act of undoing her work and demanded that she choose her new husband soon.

Having received aid from King Alcinous, Odysseus soon reached Ithaca. Upon his arrival he was met by Athena, who had disguised herself as a shepherd. She told him of the many suitors vying for Penelope's hand, of their intentions to kill Telemachus, and of Penelope's still undying love for her long-lost king. The goddess advised Odysseus to stay with the swineherd Eumaeus in order to observe the goings-on at the palace without making his presence known. To further disguise himself, Odysseus took on the appearance of a beggar.

On Athena's prompting, Telemachus abandoned the search for his father and returned home to Ithaca. He went to Eumaeus' hut first thing, since he trusted the faithful swineherd to tell him all that had happened while he was away. After Telemachus had heard all Eumaeus had to tell, he sent the swineherd to his mother to let her know of his return quietly so as not to arouse the wrath of the many suitors. Once father and son were alone in the hut, Odysseus threw off his disguise and revealed his identity. Their joy at the reunion was great, but since there was still much to do, they kept their merriment short.

The next day Odysseus, again disguised as a beggar, went to the palace, where he suffered many insults from the suitors. Upon hearing that a stranger had been treated so poorly in her home, Penelope ordered that the beggar be brought to her so she could apologize personally. Even though he yearned to reveal himself to his beloved wife, Odysseus held his tongue and instead told her of the many stories he had heard of the great Odysseus.

Penelope then told the beggar of the many suitors and how she had finally come up with a plan to rid herself of them. Before he had left for Troy, Odysseus had been renowned for his skill with the bow. He had once shot a single arrow through twelve golden rings placed in a row. Penelope told the old beggar that she would only marry the man able to string Odysseus' mighty bow (an impossible feat in itself) and duplicate her husband's feat with the golden rings.

The next day Penelope, carrying the bow, descended to the main hall of the palace, where the suitors were gathered, and told them of the decision she had come to. They all agreed to compete, and soon all were attempting to string the bow. Not one of the suitors was successful. When all had failed, the old beggar stepped forward and asked whether he might have a try. He strung the bow with no trouble at all and the suitors—and Penelope—immediately realized who was in their presence. Odysseus then shot a single arrow through the twelve rings that had been set up, thus confirming everyone's conclusions as to his identity. He then shot every one of the suitors on the spot. After twenty long years, the king of Ithaca, the mighty Odysseus, had finally come home.

Attic skyphos, 5th century B.C., showing Penelope with Odysseus in his disguise as a beggar.

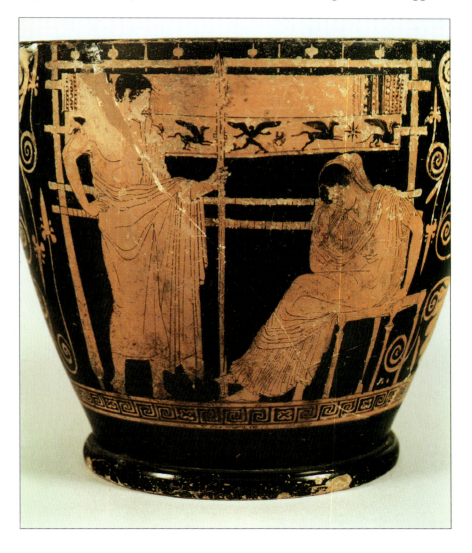

GREEK AND ROMAN NAMES

The mythology of the Romans is essentially the same as that of the Greeks. The reason for this is simple: When the Romans began taking over the land and the government of the Greeks, they also took the Greek gods. (The issue, of course, is rather more complex than this, but it is generally agreed that while the Roman imagination lent itself readily to war, politics, and practical invention, it was not so good at devising a mythology of its own.) There are certainly some differences—Mars, the Roman equivalent of Ares, is for obvious reasons more important in the Roman pantheon—and the Romans do have a number of mythological beings who belong entirely to Rome (Romulus and Remus, for example). The following table provides the Greek names of the major characters as well as their Roman equivalents.

GREEK—ROMAN	ROMAN—GREEK
Aphrodite–Venus	Apollo–Apollo
Apollo–Apollo	Bacchus–Dionysus
Ares–Mars	Ceres–Demeter
Artemis–Diana	Coelus–Uranus
Athena–Minerva	Cupid–Eros
Demeter–Ceres	Cybele–Rhea
Dionysus–Bacchus	Diana–Artemis
Eros–Cupid	Hercules–Heracles
Hades–Pluto	Juno–Hera
Hephaestus–Vulcan	Jupiter–Zeus
Hera–Juno	Latona–Leto
Heracles–Hercules	Mars–Ares
Hermes–Mercury	Mercury–Hermes
Hestia–Vesta	Minerva–Athena
Kronos–Saturn	Neptune–Poseidon
Leto–Latona	Pluto–Hades
Odysseus–Ulysses	Proserpïna–Persephone
Persephone–Proserpïna	Saturn–Kronos
Poseidon–Neptune	Ulysses–Odysseus
Rhea–Cybele	Venus–Aphrodite
Uranus–Coelus	Vesta–Hestia
Zeus–Jupiter	Vulcan–Hephaestus

BIBLIOGRAPHY

Barthell, Edward E., Jr. *Gods and Goddesses of Ancient Greece*. Coral Gables, Fla.: University of Miami Press, 1971.

Carlyon, Richard. *A Guide to the Gods: An Essential Guide to World Mythology*. New York: Quill, 1989.

Comte, Fernand. *Mythology*. Edinburgh: W & R Chambers, 1991.

Coolidge, O.E. *Greek Myths*. Illus. Edouard Sandoz. Boston: Houghton, 1949.

Cotterrell, A. *A Dictionary of World Mythology*. New York: Perigee Books, 1979.

Eliot, Alexander. *The Universal Myths*. New York: Meridian, 1976.

Evans, Berger. *Dictionary of Mythology*. New York: Laurel Books, 1970.

Fairbanks, Arthur. *The Mythology of Greece and Rome*. New York: D. Appleton, 1907.

Gayley, Charles Mills. *The Classic Myths*. Lexington, Mass.: Xerox College Publishing, 1893.

Grimal, P. *Dictionnaire de la Mythologie Grecque et Romaine*. Paris: Presses Universitaires de France, 1951.

Guthrie, W.K.C. *The Greeks and Their Gods*. Boston: Beacon Press, 1951.

Hamilton, Edith. *Mythology*. New York: Meridian, 1969.

Harvey, Sir Paul. *The Oxford Companion to Classical Literature*. Oxford: Oxford University Press, 1984.

Kaster, Joseph. *Putnam's Concise Mythological Dictionary*. New York: Perigee Books, 1990.

Lattimore, Richmond, trans. *The Iliad of Homer*. Chicago: University of Chicago Press, 1951.

Lattimore, Richmond, trans. *The Odyssey of Homer*. New York: Harper & Row, 1965.

Leach, Maria, ed. *Standard Dictionary of Folklore, Mythology and Legend*. Vols. I and II. New York: Funk and Wagnalls, 1949–1950.

Robinson, H. Spencer. *The Encyclopedia of Myths and Legends of All Nations*. London: Kaye and Ward, 1972.

Seyffert, Oskar. *Dictionary of Classical Antiquities*. New York: Meridian, 1956.

Willcock, Malcolm M. *A Companion to the Iliad*. Chicago: University of Chicago Press, 1976.

INDEX

Achilles, 21, 66, 91, 93, 94, *94*, 95, *95*, 96, *96*, 97, *98*, 105
Actaeon, 49, *49*
Admete, 83
Aeacus, 35
Aeëtes, King, 74, 75
Aegis, the, 14, 23
Aeolus, 103, 104
Agamemnon, 91, 93, 94, 97, *98*, 106
Aglaia, 64
Alcinous, King, 108
Alcmene, 77, 78
Aloidae, the, 28
Amaltheia, 14, 24
Amazons, 83, *83*
Amphitrite, 28
Amphitryon, 77, 78
Amycus, King, 73
Antikleia, 106
Antilochus, 94
Aphrodite (Venus), 20, 24, *38*, 39–43, *40*, *43*, 48, 53, 64, 88, 89, 93
Apollo, 24, *44*, 45–47, *46*, *47*, 58, *58*, 59, 70, 72, 73, 79, 91, 93, 94, 97
Apples of the Hesperides, the, 84–85
Apsyrtus, 75
Ares (Mars), 28, 40, 41, *42*, 43, *43*, 48, 52, *52*, 53, 72, 81, 83, 88, 93
Arete, Queen, 108
Argo, the, 72, 73, 74, *74*, 75
Argonauts, the, 21, *68*, 71–75, *71*, *73*, 81
Argus (boatbuilder), 72
Argus (hundred-eyed herdsman), *22*, 25
Artemis (Diana), 24, 28, *44*, 48–49, *48*, *49*, 81, *81*, 93
Ascalaphus, 72
Asphodel Fields, the, 33, 35

Atalanta, 72
Athamas, King, 60, 69, 70
Athena (Minerva), *19*, 20, 24, 46, *50*, 51–56, *52*, *53*, *54*, *55*, 60, 80, 81, 88, 93, 95, 97, 98, 101, 102, 103, 106, 108, 109
Atlantis, 29
Atlas, *18*, 57, 84, 85
Augeian Stables, the, 82
Augeias, King, 82

Brass Age, the, 21
Briseis, 94
Bronze Age, the, 21

Calais, 73
Calchis, 91, *91*
Calliope, *62*, 66, *66–67*
Calypso, 106
Cassandra, *91*
Castor, 72, 73
Centaurs, 71
Cerberus, *14*, *34*, 35, 85, *85*
Ceryneian Hind, the, 81, *81*
Chaos, 9, 10
Charon, 34, *34*, 35, 85
Charybdis, 106
Chiron, 71
Chrysaor, 28
Chryses, 91
Circe, 104, *104*, 105, *105*, 106
Cithaerian Lion, the, 78
Clio, 66, *66–67*
Coeus, 10
Cornucopia, the, 14
Creon, King, 78
Cretan Bull, the, 82–83, *82*
Cretheus, King, 71
Curetes, the, 14
Cyclopes, 10, 15, 28, *28*, 32, 102, *102*

Day, 10
Deiphobus, 95
Delphic Oracle, the, 46, 70, 79
Demeter (Ceres), 13, 29, 35, *35*, 37, 64
Demophoön, 36
Diomedes, 53, 71, 83, 91, 93, 97, 98, 101
Dione, 40
Dionysus (Bacchus), 24, 41, 59–61, *59*, *60*, *61*, 64

Echion, 72
Elysian Fields, the, 32
Elysium, 32, 35
Ephastus, 25
Ephialtes, 28, *28*
Epimetheus, 21
Erato, 67, *66–67*
Erebus, 9, 10, 33
Erichthonius, *54*, 55
Erinnyes, the, 11, 35
Eris, 41, 87–88
Eros, 9, 10, 40, *40*
Erymanthian Boar, the, 80–81
Eumaeus, 109
Euphrosyne, 64
Eurynome, 53, 64
Eurystheus, 78, 79, 80, 83, 84, 85
Eurytion, 84
Euterpe, 67, *66–67*

Furies, the, 11, 35

Gaea, 10, 11, 24, 55
Geryon, King, 83–84
Giants, 11, *11*, 28
Girdle of Hippolyte, the, 83
Golden Age, the, 18–21
Golden Fleece, the, 69–75, 81

Gorgons, 28
Graces, the, 64, *65*
Great Ancaeus, 72
Greater Ajax, 91, 94, *94*, 97, *97*, 105

Hades (Pluto), 13, 15, 27, 29, *30*, 31–35, *34*, 36, 37, *37*, 41, 61, 64, 85
Harpies, 73
Hebe, 64, *64*
Hector, 93, *93*, 94, *94*, 95, 96, *96*
Hecuba, Queen, 91
Hekatoncheires, the, 10, 15
Helen of Troy, 24, 88, *88*, 89, *89*, 90, 91, *91*, 93
Helios, 41, *43*, 106
Helle, 69, 70, *70*
Hephaestus (Vulcan), 40, 41, 43, *43*, 53–56, *53*, 81, 97
Hera (Juno), 13, 24–25, *24*, 28, 41, 44, 53, 60, 64, 70, 71, 75, 78, 83, 84, 88, 93, 94
Heracles (Hercules), 21, 24, 25, 72, *72*, 73, *76*, 77–85, *78*, *79*, *82*, *84*, *85*
Hermaphroditus, 41, *41*
Hermes (Mercury), 20, *22*, 24, 25, 40, 41, 43, *56*, 57–59, 60, 64, 70, 72, 85, *96*, 105, 106
Hesperides, the, 84–85
Hestia (Vesta), 13, 64
Hippolyte, Queen, 83
Homer, 21, 28, 40, 52, 66, 91, 96, 101
Hope, 21
Hundred-handed Ones, the, 10, 15
Hylas, 72–73, *72*
Hyperion, 10

Iapetus, 10
Idmon, 72
The Iliad (Homer), 21, 28, 40, 66, 91, 96
Ino, 60, 61, 69, 70
Io, 24–25
Iolaus, 80
Iphicles, 78
Iris, 64
Iron Age, the, 21

Jason, 71–75, *73*, *75*, 81

Krios, 10
Kronos (Saturn), 10, *10*, 11, *12*, 13–15, *14*, 24, 27, 32, 35, 40

Ladon, 84
Laestrygones, the, 104
Laocoön, *99*
Learchus, 60
Lemnian Women, the, *73*
Lernaean Hydra, the, 79–80, *80*
Lesser Ajax, 91
Leto (Latona), 46, *46*, 48
Leucon, 69
Leucothea, 61, 108
Light, 10
Love, 10

Maenads, *59*
Maia, 57
Man, creation of, 17–22
Mares of Diomedes, the, 83
Marsyas, 46, *47*
Medea, 74, 75
Medusa, 28
Megara, 78
Melpomene, 67, *66–67*
Menelaus, King, 88, *88*, 89, 90, 91, 93, *93*, 97, *98*
Metaneira, 36
Metis, 14, 15, 24, 51
Minos, King, 35, 83
Mnemosyne, 10, 66
Mount Abas, 84
Mount Artemisium, 81

Mount Atlas, 84
Mount Cyllene, 57
Mount Helicon, 78
Mount Ida, 14, 88, 94
Mount Laphystium, 70
Mount Nysa, 61
Mount Olympus, 23, 32, *32–33*, 36, 37, 41, 93
Mount Tretus, 79
Muses, the, 46, *62*, 66–67, *66–67*

Nausicaa, 108, *108*
Nemean Lion, the, 79, *79*, 82
Nephele, Queen, 69, 70
Nereids, 28, 87
Nereus, 84
Nestor, 91, 94, *98*
Nicippe, 78
Nox, 9, 10

Oceanus, 10, 15, 24, 64
Odysseus (Ulysses), 21, 28, 91, 94, 97, *97*, 98, *98*, 101–109, *102*, *103*, *105*, *107*, *108*, *109*
The Odyssey (Homer), 21, 66, 101
Olympians, 11, 15, 35
  lesser, 63–68
Oreads, 61
Orpheus, 72
Orthrus, 84
Otus, 28
Oxen of Geryon, the, 83–84

Pandalaus, 93
Pandemos, 40
Pandora, 20, *20*, 21
Paris, 88, 89, *89*, 90, 91, *91*, 93, *93*, 96, 97, *98*
Patroclus, 91, 93, 94, 95, *95*
Peleus, King, 87, *88*, 91
Pelias, 72, 75
Pelleus, 66
Penelope, 108, 109, *109*
Periclymenus, 72

Persephone (Proserpïna), 24, 35–37, *36*, *37*
Perseus, 78
Phineus, 73, 74
Phoebe, 10
Phrixus, 69, 70, *70*, 72
Plato, 40
Polydeuces, 72, 73
Polyhymnia, 67, *66–67*
Polyphemus, 28, *28*, 102, *102*, 103, *103*
Poseidon (Neptune), 13, 15, *15*, *26*, 27–29, *28*, *29*, 31, 35, 44, 55, 64, 72, 93, 94, 101, 102, 103, 108
Priam, King, 88, 89, 91, *91*, 96, *96*
Priapus, 41
Prometheus, *16*, 17, 18, *18*, *19*, 20, 21
Python, 44, 46, *46*

Rhadamanthys, 35
Rhea (Cybele), 10, 11, 13, 14, *14*, 15, 24, 35, 40, 60, 84
Rivers
  Acheron, 33, 35
  Cocytus, 34
  Lethe, 34
  Phlegethon, 34
  Scamander, 95
  Styx, 33, 34, 35, 60, 85, 96

Sappho, 67
Satyrs, 46, 58
Scylla, 106
Semele, 60, *60*
Silver Age, the, 21
Sinon, 98
Sirens, 106, *107*
Sthenelus, 78
Stymphalian Birds, the, 81–82, *82*
Symplegades, 74, *74*

Tartarus, 15, 32, 35
Teeth-Men, 74, 75

Telemachus, 108, 109
Terpsichore, 67, *66–67*
Tethis, 15
Tethys, 10, 24
Teucer, 91
Thalia, 64, 67, *66–67*
Thanatos, 31
Theia, 10
Themis, 10
Theseus, 78, *79*
Thetis, 53, 87, *88*, *92*, 93, 96
Tiresias, 105, *105*, 106
Titans, 10, 15, 17, 32, 40, 44, *46*, 57, 60, 64, 84
Trojan horse, the, 98, *99*
Trojan War, the, 53, 87–99
Twelve labors of Heracles, the, 77–85
Tyndareus, 90

Underworld, the, 32–35
Universe, creation of, 9–12
Urania, 40, *66–67*
Uranus (Coelus), 10, *10*, 11, 15, 24, 40

Zetes, 73
Zeus (Jupiter), *12*, 14, 15, *15*, 18, 20, 21, 23–24, *25*, *26*, 27, 28, 29, 31, 35, 36, 37, 40, 41, 44, 51, 52, 53, 55, 58, 59, 61, 64, 66, 73, 77, 78, 84, 88, 90, *92*, 93, 94, 106